The BILL of RIGHTS and LANDMARK CASES

The BILL of RIGHTS and LANDMARK CASES

EDMUND LINDOP

Franklin Watts
New York/London/Toronto/Sydney/1989

The author expresses his appreciation to attorney David Hardin for reading this book in manuscript and making valuable suggestions.

Photographs courtesy of:
Brown Brothers: pp. 10, 23, 32 (both), 33;
Independence National Park Collection: p. 12;
AP/Wide World: pp. 35, 52, 62, 89, 96,
104, 108, 110, 126, 134 (both); UPI/Bettmann:
pp. 40, 42, 65, 71, 86.

Library of Congress Cataloging-in-Publication Data
Lindop, Edmund.
The Bill of Rights and landmark cases / Edmund Lindop.
p. cm.
Bibliography: p.
Includes index.
Summary: Discusses landmark cases regarding the Bill of Rights.
ISBN 0-531-10790-6
1. United States—Constitutional law—Amendments—1st–10th—Cases
Juvenile literature.   2. Civil rights—United States—Cases—
Juvenile literature.   [1. United States—Constitutional law—
Amendments—1st–10th.   2. Civil rights.]   I. Title.
KF4750.L56   1989
342.73'085—dc20
[347.30285]   89-8960 CIP   AC

10.95   B+T

85438

Contents

The BILL of RIGHTS and LANDMARK CASES

One

The STRUGGLE to OBTAIN the BILL of RIGHTS

September 17, 1787, was one of the most important days in American history. On that date the delegates to the Constitutional Convention approved the new Constitution of the United States. After four grueling, emotion-charged months of arguments and compromises in hot, humid Philadelphia, the Founding Fathers had at last achieved their goal. They had created a new national government for the American people.

When the delegates had begun their deliberations in May 1787, the American states were loosely associated in a weak central government, governed by the Articles of Confederation. This Confederation had no power to tax or regulate commerce, no effective president or court system, and no way to force either the states or individuals to comply with its laws. Moreover, any attempt to make even the slightest change in the Confederation charter had to be approved by all of the states. No wonder that most of the leading American statesmen, including George Washington, Benjamin Franklin, James Madison, and Alexander Hamilton, believed the Confederation was fatally flawed and on the brink of total collapse.

The delegates gathered at Philadelphia with the express purpose of finding ways to shore up the sinking ship

The signing of the Constitution is depicted in this reproduction of a painting by Albert Herter. George Washington is seated at the desk in the center, and Benjamin Franklin is standing in the foreground at left.

of state. But they soon realized this was a futile, impossible task. So, instead of trying to add some muscle to the inept Confederation, they boldly embarked on a different course that gave birth to an entirely new framework of government, the Constitution.

Under the Constitution, the national government could tax and regulate commerce, both with foreign countries and among the states. The government was divided into three separate branches: the legislative, executive, and judicial. Each branch had clearly defined powers and also specific checks and balances to prevent the other two branches from usurping any of its powers. And a reasonable method for amending the Constitution was provided: an amendment could be added whenever it has been proposed by two-thirds of the members of each house of Congress and ratified, or approved, by three-fourths of the states.

The Constitution was one of the most remarkable documents ever produced. William Gladstone, the famous British prime minister, praised it as "the most wonderful work ever struck off at a given time and by the brain and purpose of man." [1] The Constitution replaced a fragile alliance of jealous, quarrelsome states with a government strong enough to rule effectively and efficiently. Its durability cannot be questioned. Two centuries have passed since the Constitution became the law of the land; it has endured and prevailed longer than any other country's charter of government.

Nevertheless, the Constitution would not have served the American people so long and so well if it had remained for two hundred years in its original form—without the Bill of Rights and other amendments.

Speaking in 1987, Supreme Court Justice Thurgood Marshall observed that "we must be careful when focusing on the events which took place in Philadelphia two centuries ago, that we not overlook the momentous events which followed, and thereby lose our proper sense of perspective." Marshall, the Court's first black justice, explained

The room as it appeared in 1787, when the Constitution was approved. The room can be seen today at the State House in Philadelphia.

that the Constitution was "defective from the start, requiring several amendments, a civil war, and momentous social transformation to attain the system of constitutional government, and its respect for the individual freedoms and human rights, we hold as fundamental today."[2]

WHY DIDN'T THE FOUNDING FATHERS PROVIDE A BILL OF RIGHTS?

It is logical to wonder why the brilliant politicians who assembled at Philadelphia could have drawn up the Constitution and omitted mention of such basic democratic rights as freedom of speech, freedom of religion, and the rights of people accused of crimes. Was it due to an oversight that these rights were not included in the Constitution? Or were the Founding Fathers indifferent to the concepts we cherish, such as liberty and justice for all?

The answer to both these questions is no. The failure to include a bill of rights either in the body of the Constitution or added at the end of the document was definitely not an oversight—something that had been neglected because no one at the Constitutional Convention brought it up for discussion. Elbridge Gerry, a delegate from Massachusetts, argued for a bill of rights at the convention. So did George Mason of Virginia, the author of his state's bill of rights. Gerry went so far as to make a motion calling for the inclusion of such rights in the Constitution. But when his motion was voted upon, every state delegation cast its ballot against the measure.

The Founding Fathers, many of whom had fought for American independence, believed in the concepts of liberty and justice, at least as they applied to free white men. But most of the delegates felt that their only job at the Constitutional Convention was to create a strong national government because this was the crucial issue confronting them. Considering individual rights seemed to them a diversionary tactic used by a few delegates who opposed the Constitution and wanted to see it defeated. (Both Gerry and Mason, the staunchest supporters of a bill of rights, refused to sign the Constitution.)

Moreover, many delegates felt that a national bill of rights was unnecessary. They contended that most of the states already had their own bills of rights and the national government was not given any power to infringe upon these rights. Roger Sherman of Connecticut declared, "The State Declarations of Rights are not repealed by the Constitution; and being in force are sufficient." [3]

But Sherman and his followers had not come to grips with the essential problem: The bills of rights of the various states protected individuals against only those offenses committed by that particular *state;* they did not protect individuals against offenses committed by the new *national* government or other states. The failure of the men at Philadelphia to include a bill of rights in the Constitution helped lead to an enormous upheaval that almost sounded the death knell for this great charter before it could go into effect.

RATIFICATION OF
THE CONSTITUTION

The new government could not be launched until the Constitution had been ratified by the states. Since the Founding Fathers speculated that it could be impossible to get all the states to approve the Constitution, they wisely decided that it would become the supreme law of the land as soon as it had been ratified by nine of the thirteen states. They also agreed that separate conventions would be held in each state to discuss and vote upon the fate of the Constitution. This was because state conventions would be more likely to accept the Constitution than state legislatures, whose members might not favor the new national government that would strip them of some of their powers.

Criticism of the Constitution came from other sources besides state legislators. Many Americans opposed a strong central government for various reasons. In the first place, they recently had fought the Revolutionary War to escape the tyranny of the British king, and they feared that the executive leader of the proposed new government could become a dictator with sufficient authority to oppress the citizens.

Some Americans were suspicious that the government under the Constitution would compel them to pay high taxes, which they had not been required to do by the Articles of Confederation. Furthermore, in 1787 every state had its own currency, and the value of money fluctuated widely from state to state. Debt-ridden farmers in some states had been able to convince their governments to print large amounts of paper money that helped them get higher prices for their crops. These monetary practices would end when the Constitution went into effect because it decreed a single currency and the same value of money throughout the country. This infuriated those farmers and other debtors who had relied on state printing presses to provide more money in circulation. Another concern was that the Constitution forbade tariffs on products shipped between states and required a uniform tariff rate for goods coming from foreign nations. Under the Articles of Confederation each state had set its own tariff rate on products coming from another state or a foreign country.

High on the list of complaints about the Constitution was the absence of a bill of rights, those precious personal safeguards that Elbridge Gerry and George Mason had argued for in the Constitutional Convention. The Constitution provided no protection against the establishment of a national church which all citizens might have to support. It did not guarantee that people could speak freely, belong to any groups they wished to join, or publish newspapers, magazines, and books that would not be censored by the government. It did not promise that a person accused of a crime would receive a fair trial and, if convicted, a just and humane punishment.

Those who favored the Constitution and a strong federal (national) government were called Federalists. Those who opposed the Constitution and wanted to keep the Articles of Confederation government came to be known as Antifederalists. As the ratification struggle was waged in one state convention after another, both sides flooded the public with pamphlets, articles, and speeches extolling the advantages and depicting the defects of the Constitution.

Delaware was the first state to ratify the Constitution, on December 7, 1787, and by a unanimous vote. A few days later Pennsylvania followed suit, but only after considerable opposition; one-third of the delegates voted against ratification. Next, New Jersey, Georgia, and Connecticut approved the charter.

The first five ratifying conventions had acted affirmatively, but after that the Constitution faced an uphill struggle. In three key states—Massachusetts, Virginia, and New York—the odds were against ratification. Rejection of the Constitution by these three important, populous states would spell certain doom for the new Union, which could not govern effectively without their inclusion. Even though such capable Federalists as Alexander Hamilton of New York and James Madison of Virginia led the fight for ratification in their respective states, the cause seemed nearly hopeless. Hamilton wrote to Madison, "I am very sorry . . . that your prospects [in Virginia] are so critical. Our chance of success here [in New York] is infinitely slender."[4]

Massachusetts was the first of the three key states to provide an intense battle over the Constitution. Of the convention of 355 delegates that met in January 1788, the majority were Antifederalists. Most of these dissenters opposed the Constitution because it lacked a bill of rights.

Without some concession to the widespread belief that a bill of rights was necessary, the Massachusetts Federalists realized there would not be enough votes for ratification. So they made a very shrewd decision: The Federalists themselves proposed a bill of rights in the form of amendments to the Constitution, which could be sent to the Confederation Congress along with the ratification document. Then they persuaded Governor John Hancock, who was allegedly supporting the Antifederalists, to introduce the bill of rights as his own creation. This sly strategy on the part of the Federalists won over some of the delegates who had been Antifederalists, including Sam Adams, the popular patriot and instigator of the famous Boston Tea Party.

Federalist hopes in Massachusetts now soared, but some Antifederalists threw up a roadblock. They demanded that their state's ratification not become effective until *after* the bill of rights had been adopted by a second national convention. Another convention could have opened the door to lengthy arguments and possibly to sweeping changes in the Constitution. So the Massachusetts Federalists rallied their forces to defeat this call for a second convention. Ratification was approved, but narrowly—the vote was 187 to 168.

After Maryland and South Carolina became the seventh and eighth states to ratify the Constitution, the battleground shifted to Virginia. There George Mason was joined as a leader in the Antifederalist cause by Patrick Henry and Richard Henry Lee, two of the best known men in the country. These men were not dismayed because eight of the necessary nine states had already accepted the Constitution; they knew that if Virginia, the cradle of American democracy and the site of the first legislature in the New World (the House of Burgesses), withheld its support, the new Union would be severely, perhaps mortally, wounded. "It is said eight states have adopted this plan," Henry stated. "I declare that if twelve states and a half had adopted it, I would with manly firmness, and in spite of an erring world, reject it. . . . Liberty, greatest of all earthly blessings—give us that precious jewel, and you may take everything else!''[5] Nearly every day, Henry addressed the Virginia convention, and again and again he reminded the delegates that a Constitution that did not spell out the rights of the people threatened to enslave them.

This argument impressed many delegates, and once again, as in Massachusetts, the Federalists were forced to give ground and seek a compromise. James Madison, who had not supported a bill of rights at the Constitutional Convention, now recognized that this issue no longer could be bypassed. So he agreed that Virginia should submit a bill of rights along with its ratification document, and he promised to work for their adoption as constitutional amendments when the new government convened.

Madison and his Federalist colleagues at the Virginia convention were helped by two unexpected developments. One was that Governor Edmund Randolph, who previously had opposed the Constitution, changed his mind and now supported the charter that would provide a much more effective central government. The second development was that on June 21, 1788, New Hampshire became the ninth state to ratify the Constitution, so the new Union was assured of beginning—with or without Virginia.

When the vote was finally taken at the Virginia convention, the Federalists won, 89 to 79. But the Antifederalists could claim a partial victory because Virginia coupled with its ratification a bill of rights and made the demand that it receive urgent attention from the new Congress.

During the New York convention, another lengthy, bitterly contested fight occurred, again primarily over the absence of personal rights in the Constitution. The Federalists, under the brilliant leadership of Alexander Hamilton, eked out a victory by the narrowest margin in any state—30 to 27. But the influence of the Antifederalists could not be ignored; New York also added a proposed bill of rights to its letter of ratification.

North Carolina delegates, however, were not willing to accept the Constitution and then wait to see whether Congress adopted a bill of rights. By a huge vote margin— 184 to 84—North Carolina refused to ratify the Constitution, which left this state outside the United States. Only *after* Congress took action to adopt the Bill of Rights did North Carolina join the Union.

And in Rhode Island, the anti-Constitution forces were so strong that the state did not even hold a ratifying convention before the new national government began operations. (George Washington's presidency began nearly seven months before North Carolina joined the United States and more than a year before Rhode Island became part of the Union.)

All in all, in the year following the Constitutional Convention, two states rejected the Constitution, and the ratifying conventions of five states—Massachusetts, South Carolina, New Hampshire, Virginia, and New York—submitted amendments dealing with individual rights. The demand that these rights be adopted, not just as laws but as part of the integral framework of government, was much too impassioned and too widespread to be neglected or denied.

UNFINISHED BUSINESS

When the first Congress assembled in April 1789, James Madison was one of the congressmen who recognized that the national legislature must deal with the unfinished business of adding personal rights to the Constitution. But the House of Representatives, to which Madison belonged, was in no hurry to discuss this issue and focused instead on other government business, such as import duties. Finally, on June 8, a persistent Madison reminded his colleagues, ''It cannot be a secret to the gentlemen in this House, that, notwithstanding the ratification of this system of Government . . . yet still there is a great number of our constituents who are dissatisfied with it. . . . We ought not to disregard their inclination but . . . conform to their wishes and expressly declare the great rights of mankind."[6]

Still, many other congressmen felt there were more important matters for them to consider. It was not until August 24 that the House of Representatives at last approved a bill of rights. This House bill, which was then sent to the Senate, included seventeen amendments to the Constitution.

When the Senate debated the House proposals, it reduced the number from seventeen to twelve. Among the rights it eliminated was one that Madison said was "the most valuable amendment in the whole list": It forbade the *states* from infringing on freedom of conscience, speech, press, and jury trial. The result of this deletion was that the Bill of Rights could protect persons' rights only against violations by the *national* government. It was well into the twentieth century before the Supreme Court ruled in a series of cases that the Bill of Rights could also be applied as safeguards against state violations.

On October 2, 1789, President George Washington sent the proposed twelve amendments to the states for ratification. The following month New Jersey became the first state to ratify the Bill of Rights. The New Jersey legislature, however, refused to approve the first two amendments, which actually did not pertain to individual rights. The first amendment called for one representative in the House for every thirty thousand people, and the second said that no law changing the pay of members of Congress could go into effect until after the next congressional election. Both of these amendments failed to secure ratification by three-fourths of the states, so they were dropped from the Bill of Rights.

Eleven of the fourteen states (Vermont joined the Union in March 1791) had to ratify the amendments before they could become operative. Virginia became the eleventh state to approve the Bill of Rights on December 15, 1791. Three of the other original thirteen states—Massachusetts, Georgia, and Connecticut—did not ratify the first ten amendments until many years later; they did so belatedly in 1939, on the 150th anniversary of their submission to the states.

Two

The FIRST TEN AMENDMENTS

Let us now look at the first ten amendments to the Constitution and find out why so many eighteenth-century Americans believed the Bill of Rights was absolutely essential.

THE FIRST AMENDMENT

Congress shall make no law respecting an establishment of religion, or prohibiting the free exercise thereof; or abridging the freedom of speech, or of the press; or the right of the people peaceably to assemble, and to petition the Government for a redress of grievances.

Although many colonists came to America to worship as they pleased, this did not mean they were willing to grant others the same privilege. In fact, the Massachusetts Puritans scorned religious toleration as a weakness concocted by the devil, and they assumed that any person who favored it must be "either an atheist or a heretic or a hypocrite or at best a captive of some lust." Virginia settlers, on the other hand, wanted nothing to do with the Puritan faith. They decreed that the Church of England was their established church, and they even expelled ministers from Massachusetts who came to preach.

*A copy of the Bill of Rights, the first ten
amendments to the Constitution. There were twelve
articles at one time, but the first two listed
in this document were not ratified by the states.*

By the 1760s many Americans had grown more tolerant of religions other than their own, but some of the colonies still had established churches which all of the citizens—believers and nonbelievers alike—had to support with their taxes. The notion that churches should be supported by public taxation—as happened in most European countries—died very slowly. As late as 1784 Patrick Henry proposed to the Virginia legislature that "teachers of the Christian religion" would benefit by having property owners pay a small tax to a church of their choice. Henry's motion was defeated, but only after a stinging rebuttal by James Madison. "Who does not see that the same authority which can establish Christianity, in exclusion of all other Religions," asked Madison, "may establish with the same ease any particular sect of Christians, in exclusion of all other Sects?" Madison added, "It is the duty of every man to render to the Creator such homage and such only as he believes to be acceptable to Him." [1]

Freedom of speech, of the press, of assembly, and to petition the government are closely related to freedom of religion because the right to follow one's own conscience cannot be experienced without these other rights, too. The right to believe is virtually worthless unless people are permitted to express themselves orally or in writing, and to assemble with others for the purpose of sharing ideas.

THE SECOND AMENDMENT

A well regulated Militia, being necessary to the security of a free State, the right of the people to keep and bear Arms, shall not be infringed.

Eighteenth-century Americans strongly preferred a volunteer citizen army, or militia, to a professional, standing army in peacetime. They feared that a large national army might fall under the rule of some ambitious leader who aspired to become a military dictator.

This amendment was designed to guarantee to states the right to maintain a militia. It did not restrict the power of federal and state governments to regulate private ownership of weapons, unless such regulations interfered with the militia.

THE THIRD AMENDMENT

No soldier shall, in time of peace, be quartered in any house, without the consent of the Owner, nor in time of war, but in a manner to be prescribed by law.

In colonial days British soldiers were often lodged in private homes, much against the wishes of the colonists who owned these homes. The Third Amendment was designed to prevent a recurrence of this unpleasant practice.

THE FOURTH AMENDMENT

The right of the people to be secure in their persons, houses, papers, and effects, against unreasonable searches and seizures, shall not be violated, and no Warrants shall issue, but upon probable cause, supported by Oath or affirmation, and particularly describing the place to be searched, and the persons or things to be seized.

In the years before the Revolutionary War, customs officials were armed with Writs of Assistance. These were general search warrants permitting them to hunt anywhere for smuggled goods; they did not have to secure a separate warrant for every building they entered or specify the goods they were seeking. Many colonists adamantly resented this widespread snooping by British agents.

The Fourth Amendment provides a balance between the right of privacy and the government's need to obtain evidence of a crime by requiring that, before a search, a warrant must be obtained, which specifically describes "the place to be searched, and the persons or things to be seized."

THE FIFTH AMENDMENT

No person shall be held to answer for a capital, or otherwise infamous crime, unless on a presentment or indictment of a Grand Jury, except in cases arising in the land or naval forces, or in the Militia, when in actual service in time of War or public danger; nor shall any person be subject for the same offence to be twice put in jeopardy of life or limb; nor shall be compelled in any criminal case to be a witness against himself, nor be deprived of life, liberty, or property, without due process of law; nor shall private property be taken for public use, without just compensation.

A "capital, or otherwise infamous crime" is a serious crime, such as murder. A "presentment or indictment of a Grand Jury" is an accusation by a jury of twelve to twenty-three persons that decides whether or not there is enough evidence against a person to justify bringing that person to trial for a particular crime. "Twice put in jeopardy" means that if a court has found a person not guilty of a crime, that person cannot be tried again for the same crime in another criminal court. "Nor . . . compelled . . . to be a witness against himself" means that a person can refuse to answer any question when the answer might incriminate him or her.

The "due process of law" clause is difficult to define. In general, it means that the government, in whatever it does, must act fairly and in accord with established, reasonable laws that do not infringe on the rights of citizens. "Nor shall private property be taken for public use, without just compensation" means that if the government takes private property for a public use, such as a freeway or a dam, the owner of the property must be paid a fair amount of money for the land.

THE SIXTH AMENDMENT

In all criminal prosecutions, the accused shall enjoy the right to a speedy and public trial, by an impartial jury of the State and district wherein the crime shall have been committed, which district shall have been previously ascertained by law, and to be informed of the nature and cause of the accusation; to be confronted with the witnesses against him; to have compulsory process for obtaining witnesses in his favor, and to have the assistance of Counsel for his defense.

In earlier times, both in England and to a lesser extent in colonial America, suspects could be thrown into jail, often without knowing the charges against them, and allowed to languish there for weeks or even months before their cases came to trial. Frequently they were tried by a judge without a jury, and defendants might not be allowed to cross-examine witnesses or have an attorney if they were too poor to hire one.

The Sixth Amendment, like the Fifth, provides safeguards for persons accused of crimes. It promises that the accused shall have the right to a speedy and public trial before an impartial jury. It also guarantees that every defendant shall be informed of the charges against him or her and have the assistance of a lawyer. Moreover, the accused person is permitted to confront and question (usually through an attorney) witnesses for the prosecution and to forcibly call to the stand witnesses who the defendant believes can testify in his or her behalf.

THE SEVENTH AMENDMENT

In Suits at common law, where the value in controversy shall exceed twenty dollars, the right of trial by jury shall be preserved, and no fact tried by a jury, shall be otherwise re-examined in any Court of the United States, than according to the rules of the common law.

The Seventh Amendment guarantees the right to a jury trial in civil as well as criminal cases. Civil law pertains to disputes between private parties and between private parties and the government that do not involve criminal offenses.

THE EIGHTH AMENDMENT

Excessive bail shall not be required, nor excessive fines imposed, nor cruel and unusual punishment inflicted.

"Bail" is a sum of money the accused deposits with the court. The defendant may then go free until his or her trial. The purpose is to free the accused to prepare for trial. But if the defendant runs away, the government keeps the bail money, and the accused can still be brought to trial whenever he or she is located.

The elimination of "cruel and unusual punishment" was a very important right to our forefathers. In colonial days punishment included such inhumane practices as flogging, branding, tar-and-feathering, cutting off ears, and forcing the lawbreaker to be chained to a metal ball or in the slots of wooden stocks. Cruel modes of punishment were so common that during the House debate over the Bill of Rights one congressman angrily declared that "villains often deserve whipping and perhaps having their ears cut off."

THE NINTH AMENDMENT

The enumeration in the Constitution of certain rights, shall not be construed to deny or disparage others retained by the people.

This amendment simply makes clear that the Bill of Rights does not list all of the rights of the people. Two rights not specifically stated are the right to engage in political activity and the right to privacy.

THE TENTH AMENDMENT

The powers not delegated to the United States by the Constitution, nor prohibited by it to the States, are reserved to the States respectively, or to the people.

This is sometimes called the ''states' rights'' amendment. It declares that all powers not delegated, or given, to the national government by the Constitution are reserved for, or belong to, the states or the people. The division of powers between the national and state governments is the essence of our federal system and a very important factor in the history of our republic.

Three

The SUPREME COURT, GUARDIAN of OUR RIGHTS

Most of our nation's courts may exercise the very important power of *judicial review*. This is the power to decide the constitutionality of laws and other governmental acts. If a governmental act violates some provision of the Constitution, including the amendments, it is declared *unconstitutional*, which means that the act is null and void and cannot be enforced.

Nearly all cases involving constitutional questions are first heard in lower courts—federal district courts for cases pertaining to national laws or superior courts for cases pertaining to state laws. The decisions made in these cases may be appealed to higher levels of courts and ultimately to the Supreme Court, the highest court in the land. Thus, the Supreme Court has the final authority to determine which governmental acts are constitutional and which are unconstitutional. This is an awesome responsibility to allocate to the nine members of the Supreme Court, who, in effect, are the guardians of the Constitution and its amendments.

Often these nine justices do not agree unanimously on a Court decision. Sometimes they vote 5 to 4 on a case, so the fate of an important issue may be decided by the margin of a single vote. Justices who are on the winning side of a vote are called the *majority;* those on the losing side are the *minority.* The chief justice designates one of the justices in the majority to write a *majority opinion* explaining the Court decision; other justices may also put their opinions in writing. Those who oppose the Court decision are known as *dissenters,* and their written statements about the case are *minority opinions.*

THE SUPREME COURT MAY
REVERSE ITS OPINIONS

The only way to overturn a Supreme Court decision is to add a constitutional amendment that nullifies the provision in the Constitution upon which the Court's decision was based. But this does not mean that once the Supreme Court has ruled on a case, the issue in question can never be raised again. The Supreme Court may rule one way at a certain time and later, in a similar case, hand down a much different decision.

How is it possible for the Supreme Court to "change its mind"?

In the first place, the membership of the Court changes whenever a justice retires or dies, and the new justice appointed to fill this vacancy may not have the same views as the person who is being replaced.

Secondly, new developments occur with the passage of time, and often they generate new attitudes and new concerns. So Supreme Court justices may reverse an earlier ruling because they have new and different attitudes about a particular issue.

One Supreme Court reversal with far-reaching consequences involved the Court's interpretation of whether the Bill of Rights protected citizens from state, as well as national, violations. In the 1833 case of *Barron* v. *Mayor and City Council of Baltimore,* the Supreme Court decreed that the Bill of Rights could be applied only to strike down illegal actions taken by the *national* government.

This interpretation was first seriously challenged following the Civil War, when the Fourteenth Amendment

The Supreme Court in 1865 (top left),
1921 (bottom left), and 1957 (above)

was adopted. One provision of this amendment says, ". . . nor shall any State deprive any person of life, liberty, or property, without due process of law; nor deny to any person within its jurisdiction the equal protection of the laws." Congressman John A. Bingham, the chief author of the Fourteenth Amendment, said that the due process and equal protection clauses were intended to guard the rights of all citizens against state violations. Nevertheless, for many years the Supreme Court stubbornly clung to its narrow view that the Fourteenth Amendment did not extend the Bill of Rights to *state* offenses.

Finally, in 1925, the Supreme Court began to reverse its position on this issue in the landmark case of *Gitlow* v. *New York* (see page 57). When the Court announced its decision in this case, it affirmed that freedom of speech and freedom of the press—which the First Amendment protects against violations by the national government—are also "among the fundamental personal rights and liberties protected by the due process clause of the Fourteenth Amendment from impairment by the States."

Shortly after the *Gitlow* v. *New York* (1925) decision, the Supreme Court ruled in other cases that each of the First Amendment guarantees was extended to the states by the Fourteenth Amendment. In the 1960s, the Court enlarged the scope of the Fourteenth Amendment's due process clause to cover nearly all the rest of the provisions in the Bill of Rights. So, between 1833 and 1969, the Supreme Court had moved full circle in its interpretation of whether the Bill of Rights pertained to state offenses.

Another dramatic reversal by the Supreme Court concerned racial segregation. In *Plessy* v. *Ferguson,* a decision handed down in 1896, the Court upheld (approved) a Louisiana law requiring the segregation of whites and blacks in railroad cars. The justices claimed that this law did not violate the Fourteenth Amendment's equal protection clause because the separate facilities for blacks were considered equal to those for whites.

More than fifty years later, in 1954, another landmark segregation case came before the Court. Black students had been denied admission to all-white schools in Topeka, Kansas; under Kansas law, cities with more than 15,000 residents were permitted to operate separate school systems, providing the schools were substantially equal in educational facilities. But in *Brown* v. *Board of Education of Topeka* (1954), the Supreme Court decided unanimously that segregation by race in public schools is unconstitutional. Speaking for the Court, Chief Justice Earl Warren declared, ". . . We conclude that in the field of public

Ten years after the Brown *v.* Board of Education
*case, Linda Brown stands in front of Sumner School
in Topeka, Kansas. The school's refusal to admit
Linda—then nine years old—in 1951 led to the
suit which reached the Supreme Court in 1954.
The decision came too late for Linda, but her two
sisters were able to attend Sumner School.*

education the doctrine of 'separate but equal' has no place. Separate educational facilities are inherently unequal." [1] With this momentous decision, the Supreme Court buried the separate-but-equal principle that it had vigorously supported a half century earlier.

During the long period of two hundred years since our nation was born, the Supreme Court could not have been expected to cast its decisions in concrete. Times change, and so do Court rulings. Many of the most important rulings in recent history apply to the rights of the individual.

In the following chapters you will learn how the Supreme Court, particularly in the last fifty years, has breathed life into the Bill of Rights.

Four

FREEDOM of RELIGION

Congress shall make no law respecting an establishment of religion or prohibiting the free exercise thereof.

The opening clause of the First Amendment contains not one, but two prohibitions: It forbids laws that would permit the government to establish or favor any religion, and it forbids laws that would interfere with a person's right to worship.

The responsibility of the courts has been to ensure that government remains neutral toward religion. As former Chief Justice Warren E. Burger explained in 1970, "The general principle deducible from the First Amendment and all that has been said by the Court is this: that we will not tolerate either governmentally established religion or government interference with religion."[1]

THE FREE EXERCISE OF RELIGION

The First Amendment was originally a restriction upon the national government alone. State actions affecting religion were not challenged in federal courts until the development of the doctrine that First Amendment restrictions also applied to the states through the Fourteenth Amendment. The first case raising the issue of state interference with religious practices was *Cantwell* v. *Connecticut* in 1940.

Jesse Cantwell, who belonged to the religious sect known as Jehovah's Witnesses, was trying to convert people to his faith in New Haven, Connecticut, a strongly Catholic city. Cantwell stopped two men on a sidewalk and asked their permission to play a phonograph record for them. They agreed, and Cantwell played his record, which denounced the Catholic Church as an instrument of Satan. The two men, both Catholics, were infuriated and ordered Cantwell to leave them alone. Even though no violence occurred, Cantwell was arrested and convicted of inciting others to a breach of the peace.

The Supreme Court overturned the conviction and declared that the Connecticut law pertaining to breach of the peace was too vague and left too much discretion to the officials applying it. Furthermore, the Court explained that there was no evidence that Cantwell's phonograph record, although insulting to the Catholic religion, caused any disturbance or threatened any "clear and present menace to public peace."

In the same year, 1940, the conflict between freedom of religion and governmental authority was dramatically presented to the Supreme Court in a case involving the flag salute *(Minersville School District* v. *Gobitis).* Jehovah's Witnesses refused to salute the flag because they believed that this practice was worshipping a "graven image," which was forbidden in the Bible. They quoted from the Book of Exodus that people "should have no gods besides Him." So Jehovah's Witnesses felt they could pay allegiance only to God.

In the town of Minersville, Pennsylvania, the local school board had adopted a rule requiring pupils to salute the flag daily, and students who would not take part in this ceremony were to be expelled. Lillian Gobitis, aged twelve, and her brother William, aged ten, following the instructions of their parents, both Jehovah's Witnesses, refused to salute the flag. After they were expelled from school, their father filed a lawsuit claiming that his children's free exercise of religion had been violated.

When *Minersville School District* v. *Gobitis* (1940) was appealed to the Supreme Court, the justices voted 8 to 1 to sustain the school board's rule. There are times when "religious liberty must give way to political authority," wrote Justice Felix Frankfurter for the majority. Justice Frankfurter stated that the "mere possession of religious convictions which contradict the relevant concerns of a political society does not relieve the citizens from the discharge of political responsibilities."

After the *Gobitis* ruling, the West Virginia state board of education required all schools to make flag salutes part of the daily program in which students and teachers must participate. A short time later, the seven children of Walter Barnette, a Jehovah's Witness, were expelled from West Virginia schools for refusing to salute the flag. Barnette fought for his children's rights all the way to the Supreme Court.

Only three years had passed since the *Gobitis* decision supporting compulsory flag salutes, but in *West Virginia State Board of Education* v. *Barnette,* the Court ruled in favor of Barnette. What had happened in the short interval of three years to cause the Court to reverse its position? Three justices—Hugo L. Black, William O. Douglas, and Frank Murphy—acknowledged that they had changed their minds about compulsory flag salutes. Moreover, their point of view was shared by two new justices, Wiley B. Rutledge and Robert H. Jackson, who had not been on the high bench when the *Gobitis* case was decided.

Justice Jackson, delivering the Court's majority opinion, eloquently wrote:

Walter Gobitis and his children, William and Lillian,
appear at the U.S. District Court in Philadelphia
after testifying before a judge that saluting the
American flag violated their religious principles.
The children quoted Biblical passages to support
their testimony. Two years later the Supreme Court
voted in favor of the school board's rule that
students must salute the flag.

Freedom is not limited to things that do not matter much. That would be a mere shadow of freedom. The test of its substance is the right to differ as to things that touch the heart of the existing order.

If there is any fixed star in our constitutional constellation, it is that no official, high or petty, can prescribe what shall be orthodox in politics, nationalism, religion, or other matters of opinion or force citizens to confess by word or act of faith, their faith therein.

The Amish were another religious sect that could not accept all governmental rules regulating education. A Wisconsin law compelled all students to attend school until they reached the age of sixteen, but the Amish refused to send their children to school beyond the eighth grade. Amish parents claimed that public high school education promoted secular ideas that violated their religious beliefs and scorned their tradition of living in tightly knit communities apart from outside influences.

In *Wisconsin v. Yoder,* the trial court sided with the state, maintaining that Wisconsin's compulsory attendance law was reasonable and helped prepare youth to meet the needs of a democratic society. But when the case reached the Supreme Court in 1972, the verdict was reversed on the grounds that traditional Amish beliefs could be endangered by compelling students of this sect to attend high schools. Chief Justice Warren E. Burger wrote the majority opinion, saying that a ". . . state's interest in universal education, however highly we rank it, is not totally free from a balancing process when it impinges on fundamental rights and interests, such as those specifically protected by the Free Exercise Clause of the First Amendment, and the traditional interest of parents with respect to the religious upbringing of their children."

*Amish schoolchildren in Iowa run to nearby cornfields for
protection from school officials trying to force them
to attend public schools. All but one child were able
to flee successfully. However, officials returned
later to take all the children to school on a special bus.*

Religious and moral beliefs also have conflicted with compulsory military service in times when the national security has been threatened. The draft law in World War I exempted conscientious objectors, which it identified as men belonging to a "well-recognized religious sect or organization . . . whose existing creed or principles [forbids] its members to participate in war in any form." A similar law went into effect in World War II, but it no longer required conscientious objectors to belong to a particular church or religious sect. Instead, it exempted men whose opposition to war was simply based on "religious training and belief." Shortly after World War II, Congress again changed the draft law to say that grounds for exemption were to be based on beliefs that involved "a relation to a Supreme Being."

This was the existing law in 1957 when Donald Seeger requested to be classified as a conscientious objector because he was opposed to participation in any war by reason of his religious beliefs. But Seeger refused to say whether or not he believed in a Supreme Being, and he claimed that religious convictions could be strongly held without belonging to an orthodox sect that called for a specific type of worship. Since Seeger would not acknowledge any "relation to a Supreme Being," his draft board refused to classify him as a conscientious objector. When he was ordered to be inducted into the armed forces, Seeger refused to report for duty and was tried in court for violating the selective service law. He was found guilty, but later the United States Court of Appeals overruled his conviction. The federal government then appealed the ruling to the United States Supreme Court.

Eight years after Seeger first sought exemption from military duty, the Supreme Court decided in his favor. Writing for the majority, Justice Tom C. Clark said that the "test of belief 'in a relation to a Supreme Being' is whether a given belief that is sincere and meaningful occupies a place in the life of its possessor parallel to that filled by the orthodox belief in God of one who clearly qualifies for exemption.''

Five years later, the Court went beyond *United States v. Seeger* (1965) in its interpretation of legitimate reasons for claiming exemption from military service. During the Vietnam War, Elliot A. Welsh II asked to be classified as a conscientious objector because he believed ''the taking of life—anyone's life—to be morally wrong.'' Since Welsh claimed no religious beliefs for his antiwar attitude, he was convicted and sentenced to jail for three years after he refused to be inducted into the army. But the Supreme Court reversed his sentence and declared that exemption from military duty could be granted to those persons who opposed all war on moral, as well as religious, grounds.

The Court, however, was not willing to excuse from military service those persons who were willing to participate in some wars but not in others. It decreed, in *Gillette v. United States* (1971), that a man could be drafted if his only opposition to military service was that he believed a particular war was unjust.

Another type of case involving the constitutional right to free exercise of religion came before the Supreme Court in 1986. Former Air Force Captain S. Simcha Goldman, a rabbi who had served at March Air Force Base in California, had often worn a yarmulke (scullcap) while on duty at a base hospital. He was ordered to quit doing so, however, after he wore one while testifying in a court-martial trial. While Air Force regulations generally prohibit the wearing of visible non-military apparel while in uniform, Goldman refused to stop wearing the yarmulke on duty. He asserted that this practice was a religious observance common among Orthodox and Conservative Jews. The rabbi was then threatened with court-martial and left the service, but he argued in court that the First Amendment required the Air Force to make an exception for religious attire unless it created a clear danger to discipline. Government attorneys disagreed, claiming that the armed forces did not have to permit the wearing of yarmulkes when they would detract from the uniformity sought by dress regulations.

In a 5 to 4 decision, the Supreme Court upheld the position of the Air Force in *Goldman* v. *Weinberger, Secretary of Defense* (1986). Writing for the majority, Justice William H. Rehnquist said that the Air Force rules "reasonably and evenhandedly regulate dress in the interest of the military's perceived need for uniformity" and that the application of the rules to Goldman did not violate the Constitution, even though it did limit the exercise of his religious beliefs. In dissent, Justice William J. Brennan, Jr., declared that it "surpasses belief" that military discipline would be subverted by yarmulkes.

ESTABLISHMENT OF RELIGION

Thomas Jefferson asserted that the First Amendment's prohibition against an establishment of religion was intended to build "a wall of separation between Church and State." The government, he believed, was forbidden to establish a national church or give any direct assistance to one or more religious sects.

The Supreme Court had ruled on only four church-state cases in the 160 years before 1950. Then, in just the next two decades, it handed down ten decisions, and several more cases were heard in the 1970s and 1980s. These cases involved many church-state issues, including "released time" from schoolwork for religious instruction, aid to students in parochial schools, tax exemption for religious property, prayers and Bible readings in public schools, and whether the secular or biblical interpretation of creation should be part of the school curriculum.

The "released time" issue, which first reached the Supreme Court in 1948, dealt with the widespread practice of releasing public school students from their classes in order to receive religious instruction. How often and where this religious instruction took place varied from one school district to another. The school board of Champaign, Illinois, allowed religious teachers to come into the schools once a week and teach about their faith for half an hour. Students who did not want these religious lessons were required to leave their classrooms and go to a study hall.

Vashti McCollum, the mother of a fifth grader who was the only pupil in his class who did not participate in the "released time" program, sued the school board. She maintained that religious teaching in the public schools violated the establishment clause of the First Amendment. The Supreme Court agreed with her and declared Champaign's program unconstitutional.

Four years later, the Court qualified its judgment in another "released time" case. New York City permitted students to be excused from classes for religious training, but they had to leave the school grounds once a week and go to religious centers for instruction. In *Zorach* v. *Clauson*, the Supreme Court upheld this practice. Justice William O. Douglas, writing for the majority, explained that while the First Amendment requires that there be separation of church and state "so far as interference with the 'free exercise' of religion and an 'establishment' of religion are concerned," it does not insist that church and state be separated in all other matters. "Otherwise," Douglas continued, "the state and religion would be aliens to each other—hostile, suspicious, and even unfriendly."

Douglas acknowledged the importance of religion in many people's lives and declared:

> We are a religious people whose institutions presuppose a Supreme Being. . . . [Government] respects the religious nature of our people and accommodates the public service to their spiritual needs. To hold that it may not would be to find in the Constitution a requirement that the

government show a callous indifference to religious groups. That would be preferring those who believe in no religion over those who do believe.

In cases involving government financial aid to parochial schools, the basic principle followed by the courts is that such aid is constitutional only if it primarily benefits the pupils, not the church-affiliated schools. In *Everson* v. *Board of Education of Ewing Township* (1947), the Supreme Court decided that state reimbursement of parents for the cost of transporting their children to parochial schools did not violate the First Amendment because it aided the pupils and their parents. Similarly, the Court approved a New York requirement that local school boards lend textbooks to seventh through twelfth grade students, including those attending parochial schools.

On the other hand, in 1971, the Supreme Court declared invalid a Rhode Island law authorizing supplementary salary grants to some parochial teachers. That same year it struck down a Pennsylvania law that permitted public funds to be paid to parochial schools for teachers' salaries, textbooks, and instructional materials. In both cases, decided by unanimous votes, the Court ruled that these state laws fostered "an excessive government entanglement with religion."

The question of federal aid to parochial schools surfaced again in 1985 when the Supreme Court ruled on two cases. The Court decided that public school teachers in Grand Rapids, Michigan, could not be paid from public funds to conduct courses for parochial and other private school students. The Court also invalidated a program in New York City that spent tax money to send teachers into parochial schools to enrich the teaching of secular subjects.

One of the most controversial church-state questions was whether or not voluntary prayers could be permitted in public schools. This issue aroused nationwide attention when the Supreme Court, under the activist leadership of Chief Justice Earl Warren, decided the case of *Engel* v. *Vitale* in 1962. The New York Board of Regents, an organization that ran the state's public schools, had recommended that local school districts adopt a nondenominational prayer, which could be recited voluntarily at the beginning of each school day. Students who did not want to recite the prayer were not required to do so.

The prayer was brief and concise: "Almighty God, we acknowledge our dependence upon Thee, and we beg Thy blessings upon us, our parents, our teachers, and our Country." Some of the New York school districts rejected the prayer; others accepted it and added its daily recital to their school programs.

The first challenge to this religious exercise came from the parents of ten pupils in New Hyde Park, a district that had adopted the prayer. The parents brought suit, charging that the prayer was contrary to their religious beliefs and a violation of the establishment clause of the First Amendment.

The New York courts turned down the parents' claims and upheld the use of the prayer, providing no student was compelled to recite it. But the Supreme Court, by a vote of 6 to 1, overturned the rulings of the state courts and declared use of the prayer unconstitutional. Justice Hugo L. Black wrote the opinion for the majority. He explained that the "constitutional prohibition against laws respecting an establishment of religion must at least mean that . . . it is no part of the business of government to compose official prayers for any group of the American people to recite as part of a religious program carried on by government."

The lone dissenter in this Court decision, Justice Potter Stewart, rebuked his colleagues, stating that ". . . the Court has misapplied a great constitutional principle. I cannot see how an 'official religion' is established by letting those who want to say a prayer say it." Many religious leaders agreed with Justice Stewart and condemned the activist Supreme Court for "taking God out of the schools." Public opinion surveys showed that large numbers of Americans disapproved the Court decision, and members of Congress introduced constitutional amendments to allow voluntary prayer in public schools.

No prayer amendment has yet been approved by Congress, but the issue certainly is not dead. In 1982, President Ronald Reagan asked Congress to act affirmatively on such an amendment and said that its purpose was ". . . to restore the simple freedom of our citizens to offer prayer in our public schools and institutions." [2]

The Supreme Court, however, has continued to require a strict separation of church and state. The year after the *Engel* v. *Vitale* decision, it prohibited Bible readings in public schools. In 1981, a Kentucky law that compelled every school to post a copy of the Ten Commandments in each classroom was declared unconstitutional.

More recently, in 1985, the Supreme Court ruled that an Alabama law authorizing a daily minute-long period for silent "meditation or voluntary prayer" violated the First Amendment prohibition against government establishment of religion. In this decision the Court acknowledged that a moment of silence in the schools might be lawful under a statute enacted for a neutral, nonreligious purpose. However, according to Justice John Paul Stevens, who wrote the majority opinion, the legislative intent of the Alabama law "to return prayer to the public schools is, of course, quite different from merely protecting every student's right to engage in voluntary prayer during an appropriate moment of silence during the [school] day."

The courts have had to deal with another important issue in public education: Should the schools teach the scientific theory of evolution or the biblical theory of creation—or offer the students both conflicting ideas? The evolutionary point of view, first put forth by Charles Darwin, says that life forms, including humans, evolved over millions of years. The biblical explanation, believed by many Christian Fundamentalists, is that about six thousand years ago the earth and humans were created in a process similar to that described in Genesis.

An Arkansas biology teacher had taught the theory of evolution in the 1960s, despite a 1928 state law forbidding public schools from teaching or using textbooks which discuss "the doctrine that mankind ascended or descended from a lower form of animals." The teacher was convicted of breaking the law, but the Supreme Court, by a unanimous vote in 1968, reversed his conviction and declared the Arkansas anti-evolution statute unconstitutional.

Louisiana, in 1981, adopted a law that required the public schools to teach the biblical view of creation (called "creation science") along with the theory of evolution. A high school science teacher, Donald Aguillard, along with colleagues and parents, challenged the law, and both a federal district court and an appeals court ruled the Creationism Act unconstitutional. But Louisiana Governor Edwin W. Edwards, insisting that the law reflected "balanced" teaching and was a scientific measure, not a religious one, appealed the case to the Supreme Court.

The Court announced its decision in *Edwards* v. *Aguillard* in June 1987. By a vote of 7 to 2, the justices agreed with the lower courts. Writing the majority opinion, Justice William J. Brennan, Jr., declared that the Louisiana requirement ran afoul of the First Amendment. "Creation science," he maintained, "embodies the religious belief that a supernatural creator was responsible for the creation of mankind." Therefore, Brennan concluded, the law's mandate that it be taught "advances a religious doctrine" and "seeks to employ the symbolic and financial support of government to achieve a religious purpose."

The two justices who dissented from the ruling, Chief Justice William H. Rehnquist and Justice Antonin Scalia, argued that the decision unduly restricted the ideas to which children could be exposed. The Court majority, contended Scalia, had adopted a policy of "repression" toward Christian Fundamentalists and had erred in not letting students decide "for themselves, based upon a fair presentation of the scientific evidence, about the origin of life."

In another church-state case, the issue was not the public school but the public square. Citizens in Pawtucket, Rhode Island, had displayed a Christmas crèche, or nativity scene, on government-owned property. Was this a violation of the First Amendment or a cultural symbol of peace and goodwill? The Supreme Court wrestled with this question and finally, by a 5 to 4 vote in 1984, upheld the constitutionality of the town-sponsored nativity scene. In a concurring opinion, Justice Sandra Day O'Connor explained that the Court majority had to draw a line between government actions that accommodate, or make room for, religion and those that endorse it.

Church-state relations were again the issue in a case decided by the Supreme Court in 1988. The Adolescent Family Life Act of 1981 had been passed by Congress to discourage teenage promiscuity and pregnancy. The act gave federal funds to public agencies and religious and charitable organizations for the purpose of counseling teenage girls to abstain from sexual relations.

The law was challenged in a federal district court on the grounds that public tax money was being spent to promote religious teachings, including Catholic doctrine against contraception and abortion. Examples were cited in which girls were counseled that "Jesus is your date" during teenage years and that sex is a "sin." The district court judge struck down the law as a violation of the First Amendment ban on "laws respecting an establishment of religion."

The Supreme Court, however, by a 5 to 4 vote, reversed the lower court decision and upheld the law. Writing for the majority, Chief Justice William H. Rehnquist said that the fact that grants pay for counseling "on questions such as premarital sex, abortion and the like" that

*The controversial nativity scene on display
in Pawtucket, Rhode Island's public park prior
to the Supreme Court's decision allowing the
town-sponsored Christmas crèche to remain.*

"happen to coincide with the religious views" of some groups receiving the grants was not enough by itself to prove "that the grants are being used in a way as to have a primary effect of advancing religion." But the Court conceded that there might be particular groups that were using their government funds mainly to teach religious dogma. So the case was returned to the district court with instructions to order that the grants of violators be canceled.

The four Supreme Court justices who disagreed with the majority decision maintained that the violations were so widespread as to justify ending all grants to religiously affiliated groups.

Five

FREEDOM of SPEECH

Congress shall make no law . . . abridging the freedom of speech.

Freedom of speech is one of our most precious rights, yet it has raised many questions. Should speech that endangers the security of our country be permitted? Should remarks that might lead to violence be allowed? Should freedom of speech apply only to those who voice opinions that most people agree with? Or should it be for all people, even for those who hold opinions most of us despise? And should the use of nonverbal symbols, such as burning the American flag or wearing controversial armbands, be protected under the freedom of speech clause of the First Amendment?

SPEECH AND SEDITION

It was not until after World War I that the Supreme Court began to hear cases involving sedition, which is language or conduct inciting rebellion against the authority of the government. The first notable decision was *Schenck* v. *United States* (1919). In 1917, while American soldiers were fighting in France, the general secretary of the Socialist party, Charles T. Schenck, together with other party members, mailed fifteen thousand leaflets to young men urging them to resist the draft. Schenck and his colleagues were arrested for violating the Espionage Act of 1917 and charged with conspiring to cause insubordination in the armed forces, obstructing the draft, and using the mails unlawfully.

The Socialist circulars had claimed that the Conscription Act was unconstitutional and that those wishing to oppose the draft had the right to do so. When Schenck and his associates were convicted, they appealed on the grounds that their rights to free speech had been denied.

However, the Supreme Court was unanimous in upholding their convictions. Justice Oliver Wendell Holmes, Jr., in explaining the Court's opinion, said that "in many places and in ordinary times the defendants in saying all that was said in the circular would have been within their constitutional rights." But, he observed, these were not ordinary times; the nation was at war and the Socialist circular obviously was produced to interfere with the war effort. "The most stringent protection of free speech," Holmes wrote, "would not protect a man in falsely shouting fire in a crowded theatre and causing a panic." The Court concluded that Schenck's leaflets were used in circumstances that would create "a clear and present danger" which "Congress has the right to prevent."

The *clear and present danger* test has been used often in deciding whether speech must be limited. In another 1919 case involving activities during World War I, Jacob Abrams and four friends had been arrested in New York City for printing and throwing out of windows two sets of inflammatory pamphlets. One pamphlet, written in English, protested the sending of American troops to Russia in 1918, described President Woodrow Wilson as a coward and hypocrite, and proclaimed that ". . . there is only one enemy of the workers of the world and that is CAPITALISM." The second leaflet, printed in Yiddish, urged workers in munitions factories to engage in a general strike, disavow their confidence in the United States government, and "spit in the face the false, hypocritic, military propaganda which has fooled you so relentlessly, calling forth your sympathy, your help [in] the prosecution of the war."

In *Abrams* v. *United States,* the Supreme Court ruled that the purpose of the two sets of leaflets was to incite sedition and revolution, and upheld the defendants' prison sentence of twenty years. But two justices dissented— Holmes and Louis D. Brandeis. Justice Holmes asserted that the actions of Abrams and the other defendants had not created a "clear and present danger" to national security. The chief difference between the *Schenck* and *Abrams* cases, he believed, was that Schenck's circular had been mailed to young men advising them to defy the draft, while Abrams simply had thrown pamphlets indiscriminately out of windows. Holmes maintained that "Congress certainly cannot forbid all efforts to change the mind of the country."

Then, in his famous dissenting opinion, Holmes wrote this often-quoted, eloquent statement about the nature of free expression:

> . . . the best test of truth is the power of the thought to get itself accepted in the competition of the market. . . . That at any rate is the theory of our Constitution.
>
> It is an experiment, as all life is an experiment. . . . While that experiment is part of our system, I think that we should be eternally vigilant against attempts to check the expression of opinions that we loathe and believe to be fraught with death, unless they so imminently threaten immediate interference with the lawful and pressing purposes of the law that an immediate check is required to save the country.

You recall that in *Gitlow* v. *New York* (1925), the Supreme Court, for the first time, decreed that a First Amendment protection was extended to state actions by the Fourteenth Amendment. But even though his case set this tremendously significant precedent, Benjamin Gitlow still went to prison. A member of the left-wing faction of the Socialist party, Gitlow was convicted under New York's criminal anarchy law because he had printed and distributed sixteen thousand copies of a manifesto that called for the overthrow of the state by the proletariat, or poorest class of workers.

Gitlow appealed his conviction to the Supreme Court, arguing that the New York law unconstitutionally limited his rights of free speech and free press, and that he had taken no overt action that would present a clear and present danger of the revolution he wrote about. The Supreme Court conceded there was no evidence of a clear and present danger, but, nevertheless, upheld Gitlow's conviction.

Writing for the majority, Justice Edward T. Sanford claimed that the First Amendment does not protect those who abuse freedom of expression by statements harmful "to the public welfare, tending to corrupt public morals, or disturb the public peace. . . . Such utterances, by their very nature, involve danger to the public peace and to the security of the State. They threaten breaches of the peace and ultimate revolution." Sanford declared that a state has the "right of self preservation" and that this right could be threatened when "[a] single revolutionary spark may kindle a fire that, smoldering for a time, may burst into a sweeping and destructive conflagration." Thus the state could "extinguish the spark without waiting until it has enkindled the flame or blazed into the conflagration."

In 1940, Congress passed the Smith Act, which made it a crime to advocate or teach the overthrow of any government in the United States by force or any type of violence. It also became a crime to print, distribute, or publicly display any material that supported such sedition. If two or more people gathered to commit any of these offenses, they could be charged with criminal conspiracy.

The Smith Act was largely dormant during World War II, but it became the focus of nationwide attention when the Cold War between the Soviet Union and the United States escalated in the late 1940s. This was a period when many Americans genuinely feared that Communist sympathizers in our country were plotting treasonable acts against the government. Eleven leaders of the Communist party in the United States were arrested in 1948 under the Smith Act and charged with conspiring to teach the overthrow of the government by force and violence. Their highly publicized trial in a federal district court lasted nine months. The verdict was that the defendants were guilty.

The Communist leaders appealed their case to the Supreme Court, alleging that a "conspiracy to advocate a revolution" was not the same as actually starting a revolt. They insisted that it was unconstitutional to punish them for their ideas, since these ideas were not accompanied by seditious acts.

Finally, in 1951, the Supreme Court, by a 6 to 2 vote, decided against the defendants. In *Dennis* v. *United States,* Chief Justice Fred M. Vinson expressed the opinion that "overthrow of the government by force and violence is certainly a substantial enough interest for the Government to limit speech. . . . for if a society cannot protect its very structure from armed internal attack, it must follow that no subordinate value can be protected."

Justices Hugo L. Black and William O. Douglas dissented. Black pointed out that the eleven Communist leaders had not been accused of an actual attempt to overthrow the government but only with agreeing "to assemble and to talk and to publish certain ideas at a later date. The indictment is that they conspired to organize the Communist Party and to use speech or newspapers . . . to teach and advocate the forcible overthrow of the Government.

No matter how it is worded, this is a virulent form of prior censorship of speech and press, which I believe the First Amendment forbids.''

The *Dennis* decision encouraged the federal government to prosecute other American Communists, and between 1951 and 1956 more than 120 so-called ''second-string'' Communists were arrested and convicted. But by 1957, when the Supreme Court agreed to review the convictions of fourteen persons charged with violating the Smith Act, there were four new members of the Court. While the majority of justices did not believe that the Smith Act should be overturned, they narrowed its scope. In *Yates* v. *United States* (1957), they reversed the convictions of the fourteen Communists. Delivering the majority opinion, Justice John Marshall Harlan emphasized the difference between advocating a seditious doctrine and performing an unlawful act. The Court now held that the mere belief in revolutionary ideas was ''too remote from concrete action'' to justify conviction.

''FIGHTING WORDS'' AND PUBLIC SAFETY

New Hampshire passed a law that declared: ''No person shall address any offensive, derisive or annoying word to any other person who is lawfully in any street or other public place, nor call him by any offensive or derisive name. . . .''

Chaplinsky, a member of Jehovah's Witnesses, was distributing the literature of his sect on the streets of Rochester, New Hampshire. Some of the people he encountered were angered when he denounced other religions as ''a racket.'' The crowd grew restless, a disturbance occurred, and a traffic officer took Chaplinsky to the police station. On the way they met Rochester's city marshal, and Chaplinsky said to him: ''You are a God damned racketeer. A damned Fascist and the whole government of Rochester are Fascists or agents of Fascists.''

Chaplinsky was convicted of breaking the state law making it a crime to call another person ''offensive and derisive names'' in public. Carrying his case all the way to the Supreme Court, the convicted man maintained that the New Hampshire law violated the First Amendment because it punished speech alone. The Supreme Court, however, unanimously sustained Chaplinsky's conviction and emphasized that speech has certain limitations. Justice Frank Murphy, writing the Court opinion in *Chaplinsky* v. *New Hampshire* (1942), explained:

> . . . it is well understood that the right of free speech is not absolute at all times and under all circumstances. There are certain well-defined and narrowly limited classes of speech, the prevention and punishment of which has never been thought to raise any Constitutional problem. These include the lewd and obscene, the profane, the libelous, and the insulting or ''fighting'' words— those which by their very utterance inflict injury or tend to incite an immediate breach of the peace.

The Supreme Court, however, has not always defined ''fighting words'' in the same way. In 1949, the justices were confronted with *Terminiello* v. *Chicago,* a case somewhat similar to *Chaplinsky.* Arthur Terminiello had given a speech in Chicago in which he savagely attacked Jews, blacks, and the administration of President Franklin D. Roosevelt.

When Terminiello spoke, the auditorium was filled with over eight hundred people, including many who belonged to a right-wing, anti-Semitic group. Outside the auditorium a large angry crowd gathered to protest the meeting. Bricks and bottles were rained through the windows as Terminiello delivered his message of hate. The police were unable to prevent several fierce clashes between the hatemonger's supporters and enemies.

Terminiello was arrested and convicted of inciting a breach of the peace in violation of a Chicago ordinance. The Supreme Court, voting 5 to 4, reversed his conviction chiefly on the ground that the trial judge had improperly instructed the jury that a breach of the peace could be committed by speech that "stirs the public to anger, invites dispute, brings about a condition of unrest, or creates a disturbance."

Speaking for the majority, Justice William O. Douglas declared:

> . . . a function of free speech under our system of government is to invite disputes. It may indeed best serve its high purpose when it induces a condition of unrest, creates dissatisfaction with conditions as they are, or even stirs people to anger. . . . That is why freedom of speech, though not absolute . . . is nevertheless protected against censorship or punishment, unless likely to produce a clear and present danger of a serious substantive evil that rises above public inconvenience, annoyance, or unrest.

Two years later the Supreme Court took a still different position when it dealt with the case of Irving Feiner, a college student, who stood on a large wooden box and addressed a crowd on a street corner in Syracuse, New York. In the course of his speech, Feiner made vicious remarks about President Harry S. Truman, the American Legion, and the mayor of Syracuse.

The street crowd was restless, and there was some pushing and shoving. After Feiner had been speaking for about twenty minutes, one of the enraged listeners told a police officer to get Feiner off the wooden box or he would pull him off himself. One of the officers asked Feiner to

The Reverend Arthur Terminiello reads the Supreme Court's ruling in his favor—clearing him of disorderly conduct arising from a speech he gave three years earlier in which he attacked Jews, blacks, and President Roosevelt's administration.

quit talking so that the crowd could be dispersed, but Feiner refused. After he refused a second and third request to stop speaking, the officer arrested him for disorderly conduct.

Feiner was found guilty and sentenced to thirty days in jail. When his appeal was heard by the Supreme Court in 1951, the justices voted 6 to 3 to uphold his conviction. Writing the majority opinion, Chief Justice Fred M. Vinson explained that the police had not acted to suppress speech but to preserve order. "It is one thing to say that the police cannot be used as an instrument for the oppression of popular views," Vinson observed, "and another to say that, when as here the speaker . . . undertakes incitement to riot, they are powerless to prevent a breach of the peace."

SYMBOLIC SPEECH

The Supreme Court has had to decide whether certain nonspoken symbols fall under the free speech protection of the First Amendment. Two such cases reached the Court in 1968, at a time when there was intense opposition to the Vietnam War. One case, *United States* v. *O'Brien*, concerned a young man who had burned his draft card to protest the war and the draft. He claimed this was an expression of symbolic speech permitted by the First Amendment. The Court disagreed, contending that conscription during wartime was an essential part of the government's need to maintain armed forces.

The second case, *Street* v. *New York,* involved a man who had burned an American flag. Street had just heard a news report telling about the shooting of James Meredith, a Southern civil rights leader. Infuriated, he took a flag from his house, walked to an intersection and, in the presence of about thirty people, burned it. He said angrily, "If they let that happen to Meredith, we don't need an American flag.''

Street was convicted under a New York law making it a crime to mutilate the flag or to cast contempt on it either by words or acts. In a 5 to 4 decision, the Supreme Court reversed Street's conviction on the ground that he was "punished merely for speaking defiant or contemptuous words about the flag." The Court held that New York's law infringed on the First and Fourteenth Amendments because it punished Street for expressing his opinion about the flag.

The following year the Supreme Court heard a case concerning students in Des Moines, Iowa, who had worn black armbands to school as a symbolic protest against the Vietnam War. The principals of the Des Moines schools had learned about this activity before it occurred and had agreed that any student wearing a black armband would be told to remove it. A student who refused would be suspended and not allowed to return to school while wearing the armband. The principals made this regulation because they feared that the armbands might create disturbances and cause student demonstrations.

Nevertheless, thirteen-year-old Mary Beth Tinker, along with her brother and a friend, wore those armbands to school in December 1965. When the students refused to take them off, they were suspended. Through their parents, the students then sued in court to establish their First Amendment right to wear the armbands.

When the case reached the Supreme Court in 1969, the justices voted 7 to 2 in favor of the students. Justice Abe Fortas wrote the majority opinion, declaring that neither students nor teachers "shed their constitutional rights to freedom of speech or expression at the schoolhouse gate."

The *Tinker* v. *Des Moines Independent Community School District* (1968) decision played a role in a much later case the Supreme Court heard in 1986. Matthew Fraser,

*Mary Beth Tinker and her brother, John, display
the black armbands they wore in protest of the
Vietnam War and for which they, and their brother,
sister, and a fifth youth were suspended from school.*

a high school senior, had been suspended from school for giving a sexually suggestive speech. While Fraser said no obscene words, he did make several sexual allusions in his talk. Fraser went to court, claiming that his right to express symbolic speech had been denied. A federal district court and an appeals court both ruled for the student, basing their decisions on the precedent set by *Tinker*. But the Supreme Court, by a 7 to 2 vote, disagreed. Chief Justice Warren E. Burger scolded the lower courts for "ignoring the marked distinction between the political message of the armbands and the sexual content of the student's speech in this case." Burger contended that "the First Amendment does not prevent the school officials from determining that to permit vulgar and lewd speech such as [Matthew Fraser's] would undermine the school's basic educational mission."

In dissent, Justice John Paul Stevens, joined by Justice Thurgood Marshall, charged that the Court majority had applied moral standards to this case that were much too prudish for the 1980s. Stevens reminded his colleagues that the phrase, "Frankly, I don't give a damn," in the movie *Gone With the Wind*, was considered shocking "when I was a high school student."

Freedom of speech was again the chief issue in a 1987 case pertaining to the solicitation of pamphlets. This case arose in July 1984, when an officer at Los Angeles International Airport told Avi Snyder, a minister for Jews for Jesus, that he could not pass out free religious leaflets in the airport terminal. Because of the large crowds at the busy airport and the possibility that solicitors could block corridors or harass passengers, the board of airport commissioners had adopted a policy in 1983 that the terminal area "is not open for First Amendment activities by any individual or entity."

Although no legal action was taken against Snyder, he initiated court action to prove that his constitutional rights had been violated. His efforts were successful, for the

Supreme Court ruled unanimously that the airport regulation was unconstitutional. Justice Sandra Day O'Connor, speaking for the Court, declared that the ban on all "First Amendment activities" in the airport terminal could be read to "prohibit even talking and reading or the wearing of campaign buttons or symbolic clothing. . . . No conceivable government interest," O'Connor concluded, "would justify such an absolute prohibition of speech."

Six

FREEDOM of the PRESS

Congress shall make no law . . . abridging the freedom . . . of the press.

One of the chief differences between a democracy and a dictatorship is the role of the media in communicating information. In a democracy, the media, except for a few limitations you will read about, is free to express ideas without fear of censorship. In a dictatorship, the government controls and censors all sources of information—books, newspapers, magazines, plays, movies, and television.

PRIOR RESTRAINT

Prior restraint is one form of censoring the press. This is the practice of restraining, or not permitting, a publication to be printed. For many years the government of England exercised prior restraint through its power to license publications, and eighteenth-century Americans did not want this form of censorship. This is one reason why the protection of a free press was included in the First Amendment.

Near v. *Minnesota* (1931) was the first case in which the Supreme Court ruled on prior restraint of the press. At issue in this case was the so-called Minnesota Gag Law, which gave the state the power to shut down a publication held to be a "public nuisance."

Jay M. Near was one of the publishers of the *Saturday Press,* a weekly newspaper which, in a series of articles, charged that local government officials had failed to suppress "a Jewish gangster" who allegedly operated gambling, racketeering, and bootlegging rings in Minneapolis. The newspaper printed obviously anti-Semitic stories and scandalous charges that it could not prove, so the county attorney obtained from a judge a temporary restraining order to cease publication of this "public nuisance." The lower court and the state supreme court agreed that the *Saturday Press* should not be published because it ran afoul of the Minnesota Gag Law.

But the Supreme Court, in a 5 to 4 decision, declared that the Minnesota statute was unconstitutional. Writing for the majority, Chief Justice Charles Evans Hughes said that there can be no censorship of a newspaper before publication. He added, however, that there might be punishment after publication if individuals defamed by the paper could prove in court that the newspaper had violated the libel laws.

Another type of prior restraint surfaced in the 1936 case of *Grosjean* v. *American Press Company.* The legislature of Louisiana, coaxed by Governor Huey Long, passed a law that imposed a tax of 2 percent on the gross receipts of newspapers that had a weekly circulation of more than 20,000 copies. The law was written so that the tax fell nearly entirely on those newspapers that opposed the administration of Governor Long.

The newspapers went to court to stop enforcement of this law on the grounds that the tax violated freedom of the press. When the Supreme Court heard the case, it ruled unanimously that the Louisiana tax law was unconstitutional. This tax, explained Justice George Sutherland, was not decreed for the purpose of supporting the government, but instead it was meant to limit the circulation of information necessary for a free people and a free government.

In June 1971, the Supreme Court had to decide a landmark case in which President Richard M. Nixon and the Justice Department attempted to prevent the publication of some of the so-called Pentagon Papers. The case arose after the *New York Times* began printing a series of articles based on a classified Defense Department study of America's involvement in the Vietnam War. This secret information was given to the *Times,* and later to the *Washington Post,* by Daniel Ellsberg, an antiwar protester who previously had worked for the Defense Department.

The *Times* asserted that it was important for the American people to know the full story of their country's controversial role in the war, including those passages that discussed how some government leaders had deceived the public. But lawyers for President Nixon and the Justice Department insisted that publishing the Pentagon Papers would endanger national security and impede American foreign relations, which sometimes must be conducted secretly. So the government lawyers received from a federal judge a temporary restraining order that prevented both the *Times* and the *Post* from publishing the rest of the classified information.

The attention of people throughout the country was riveted on this classic struggle between the First Amendment and the executive branch of our government. Without delay, the newspapers carried their cases to the Supreme Court. On June 30, 1971—only fifteen days after the government had first tried to censure the *Times*—the Court announced that it had voted 6 to 3 in favor of the newspapers. The nine justices each wrote a separate opinion on this important case. In a statement concurring with the majority, Justice Hugo L. Black said, "Both the history and language of the First Amendment support the view that the press must be left free to publish news, whatever the sources, without censorship, injunctions, or prior restraints."

A newspaper worker celebrates the first edition of the Washington Post *after the Supreme Court's decision to allow the paper to resume publication of a top-secret Pentagon study of the Vietnam War.*

Justice John Marshall Harlan, one of the three dissenters, felt that the Court moved too quickly in reaching its decision. Harlan declared that he could "not believe that the doctrine prohibiting prior restraints reaches to the point of preventing courts from maintaining the status quo long enough to act responsibly in matters of such national importance. . . ."

Another prior restraint case was decided by the Supreme Court in 1988. The case stemmed from a local law giving the mayor of Lakewood, Ohio, the authority to issue or deny permits for placing newspaper vending boxes on Lakewood streets. The law did not specify on what basis the mayor was to reach this decision.

Publishers of the *Cleveland Plain Dealer,* who had been denied permission to use street boxes in Lakewood for selling their papers, brought suit, contending that the local law violated the First Amendment protection of freedom of the press. Attorneys for Lakewood argued that this was a property rights case and that no one had a right to use city property without permission.

By a vote of 4 to 3, the Supreme Court decreed that while city officials may regulate where newspaper boxes are permitted on public streets, they do not have the authority to decide which newspapers are sold there. Justice William J. Brennan, Jr., expressing the opinion of the majority, said that the Lakewood law was unconstitutional because it allowed newspapers to be punished if they opposed the mayor. "In the area of free expression," Brennan wrote, "a licensing statute placing unbridled discretion in the hands of a government official or agency constitutes a prior restraint and may result in censorship."

In dissent, Justice Byron R. White asserted that if a city can prohibit soft drink vending machines on city property, it could also prohibit newspaper vending machines. He said that the First Amendment does not give newspaper publishers the right "to cordon off a portion of the sidewalk in an effort to increase the circulation of their papers."

There has long been the possibility of conflict between the First Amendment's right to freedom of the press and the Sixth Amendment's promise of a fair trial by an impartial jury. In *Bridges* v. *California* (1941), the Supreme Court established the standard that was to be followed in deciding cases that pitted these two amendments against each other: publication was to be limited only where it would present a clear and present danger to the judicial process.

At times the press has been judged to have too much influence over the outcome of a trial. One such case dealt with the murder of a woman in Cleveland, Ohio, in 1954. Her husband, Dr. Sam Sheppard, was charged with the murder. There was an enormous amount of pretrial publicity; reporters interviewed key witnesses and wrote stories based on data supplied by the prosecuting attorneys that were damaging to Sheppard. During the trial, a large army of reporters practically took over the courtroom, badgering jurors, witnesses, and lawyers. Many journalists announced Sheppard's guilt in the newspapers long before the jury had reached this verdict.

Twelve years later, in 1966, the Supreme Court reversed this conviction, claiming that Sheppard's rights as a defendant had been violated. The Court's decision was based on the failure of the trial judge to protect Sheppard from overwhelming, one-sided publicity that made it impossible for him to receive a fair trial and also because of extreme disruptions in the trial that were caused by the press.

As in the *Sheppard* case, an event that occurred on October 18, 1975, involved a sensational crime that was reported in newspaper headlines and on television broadcasts. Six members of the Henry Kellie family were found murdered in their home in Sutherland, Nebraska.

Ervin Charles Simants was arrested and charged with committing the brutal murders. This crime attracted such wide press coverage that the prosecuting and defense attorneys jointly asked the judge for an order restricting the flow of news in order to guarantee the defendant a fair trial. The judge, remembering the *Sheppard* case, agreed with the attorneys and issued a "gag order" on the day of the preliminary hearing. Even though that hearing was held in open court, the press was prohibited from reporting any of the testimony or evidence presented. This order was to continue in effect until the jury was chosen.

Several newspaper publishers protested that the restrictive gag order infringed on the freedom of the press. In 1976, the Supreme Court had to decide whether this gag order was constitutional. The Court agreed unanimously that it was unconstitutional; four opinions were written because of the importance of this free press-fair trial confrontation. Chief Justice Warren E. Burger admitted that this issue was not an easy one to decide because the "authors of the Bill of Rights did not undertake to assign priorities as between the First Amendment rights and Sixth Amendment rights, ranking one as superior to the other." Nonetheless, he explained, we have developed a tradition that opposes censorship or prior restraints on the press, and the trial judge could have found means other than a gag order to protect the rights of the accused.

A Supreme Court ruling usually sets a *precedent,* or standard, for courts to follow in similar cases. In *Gannett Co., Inc.* v. *DePasquale* (1979), the Court decreed that if the defendant, the prosecution, and the judge agreed, a pretrial hearing about the legality of evidence could be closed to the press and the public. *Gannett* left it unclear whether trials as well as pretrial hearings could be closed. As a result, in the year following this decision, there were 160 closed criminal proceedings—126 were pretrial hearings and 34 were actual trials. Clearly, the precedent established by *Gannett* was being interpreted by the lower courts in such a way as to severely restrict freedom of the press.

In 1980, the Supreme Court took advantage of another case to undo the *Gannett* precedent of closing criminal courts. A judge in a Richmond, Virginia, murder case had ordered that the courtroom be kept clear of all observers except the witnesses when they testified. Richmond newspapers challenged this ruling, and, by a 7 to 1 majority, the Supreme Court sided with the newspapers. Chief Justice Burger, writing for the majority, said, "In guaranteeing freedoms such as those of speech and press, the First Amendment can be read as protecting the right of everyone to attend trials. . . ." The only exception to public trials, Burger declared, would be those in which the defense or the prosecution can convince the judge that there is a compelling need to close the proceedings.

The question of whether a criminal trial could be televised confronted the Supreme Court in 1981. A Florida law permitted television coverage of judicial proceedings subject to the control of the presiding judge. Two defendants in a Miami, Florida, criminal case were convicted by a jury despite their objections that television broadcasts of parts of the proceedings denied them a fair and impartial trial. In *Chandler* v. *Florida* (1981), the Supreme Court ruled unanimously that the defendants had failed to prove that the television coverage of their case had affected the jury's verdict. "To demonstrate prejudice in a specific case," said Chief Justice Burger, "a defendant must show something more than juror awareness that the trial is such as to attract the attention of broadcasters."

OBSCENITY AND CENSORSHIP

Obscenity is a term used to describe something that is indecent, lewd, or offensive in behavior, expression, or appearance. While the First Amendment guarantees freedom of the press and speech, it says nothing about protecting obscenity. But since 1957, no First Amendment question has divided the Supreme Court more than the censorship and suppression of allegedly obscene literature or art. This is because the Court in each case must weigh the individual's right of free expression against society's responsibility to protect the morals and welfare of the community. Part of the problem is that it is difficult to decide what is obscene. Some people might read a book or look at a film and call it vulgar and lewd. Others might not be offended by the same book or movie and may say that it has creative, literary, or artistic merit.

The Court first tried to define obscenity in the 1957 case of *Roth* v. *United States*. Samuel Roth had been convicted in New York City of violating the federal obscenity law by mailing obscene books, circulars, and advertising material. By a 6 to 3 vote, the Court upheld Roth's conviction, and Justice William J. Brennan, Jr., expressed the opinion of the majority when he declared that ". . . implicit in the history of the First Amendment is the rejection of obscenity as utterly without redeeming social importance." Then Brennan went on to say that the test for deciding if materials are obscene should be "whether to the average person, applying contemporary community standards, the dominant theme of the material taken as a whole appeals to prurient [sexually arousing] interest."

The Supreme Court continued to struggle with the obscenity issue, sometimes upholding convictions from lower courts and other times reversing them. Between 1957 and 1968, the justices decided thirteen obscenity cases and wrote fifty-five separate opinions. Since there was no unanimous agreement as to what was obscene, each justice had to draw his own conclusions about which questionable materials should or should not be protected by the First Amendment. For example, Justice Potter Stewart explained that the only definition of obscenity that he could offer was "I know it when I see it."

In *Miller* v. *California* (1973), the Supreme Court ruled, by a 5 to 4 vote, that individual states may ban books, magazines, films, or plays if they are offensive to local standards. Chief Justice Warren E. Burger, writing the majority opinion, said, ". . . to equate the free and robust exchange of ideas and political debate with commercial exploitation of obscene material demeans the grand conception of the First Amendment and its high purposes in the historic struggle for freedom.'' Then Burger presented specific guidelines for determining what is obscene. Material is obscene, he reasoned, (1) if the average person, applying contemporary community standards, would find the work as a whole appealing to prurient feelings; (2) if the work depicts or describes sexual conduct in a strongly offensive way; and (3) if the work as a whole lacks serious literary, artistic, political, or scientific value.

These guidelines became the yardstick by which later obscenity cases were judged. But they did not satisfy everyone. Justice William O. Douglas, who cast a dissenting vote in the *Miller* case, asserted that ''since 'obscenity' is not mentioned in the Constitution or Bill of Rights,'' it cannot constitutionally be punished. Justice William J. Brennan, Jr., another dissenter, was concerned about the need to decide whether a work has serious value. Before this case, he said, ''the protections of the First Amendment have never been thought limited to expressions of *serious* literary or political value.''

Other critics of the *Miller* guidelines complained that it is difficult to select ''average'' persons as jurors who must decide whether a work as a whole appeals mainly to sexual feelings. They also were concerned that ''community standards'' might deprive people in one place from seeing a movie or reading a book that is legally available in another place. Clearly, the guidelines proposed in *Miller* raised almost as many questions about obscenity as they answered.

Finally, in a 1987 case, the Supreme Court made a major change in the *Miller* rules for judging what is obscene. An Illinois court had convicted two bookstore clerks for selling magazines that the jury believed would be considered obscene by adults in their state. By a 6 to 3 vote, the Supreme Court reversed the obscenity convictions and said that juries must now apply a national, not state or local, standard in deciding whether a work has redeeming value. "The proper inquiry," wrote Justice Byron R. White for the majority, "is not whether an ordinary member of a given community could find [some] value in allegedly obscene material, but whether a reasonable person would find such value in the material, taken as a whole." White concluded that "the ideas a work represents need not obtain majority approval to merit protection" under the First Amendment.

LIBEL

Libel is a written, printed, or pictorial statement that damages a person by defaming his or her character or reputation. *Defaming* is generally defined as falsely communicating information that injures a person's reputation by lowering the community's regard for that person or by otherwise holding an individual up to hatred, contempt, or ridicule.

A landmark libel case, *New York Times Co.* v. *Sullivan,* reached the Supreme Court in 1964. The civil rights struggle of the 1960s raised the question of whether a public official could receive damages for libel from those who made defamatory charges about his conduct in office.

On March 29, 1960, a full-page advertisement appeared in the *New York Times* signed by sixty-four people, including a number of Southern black clergymen. The ad referred to the widespread nonviolent demonstrations by Southern blacks to affirm their "right to live in human dignity as guaranteed by the U.S. Constitution and the Bill of Rights." Then the advertisement went on to say that the blacks had been confronted by a "wave of terror" instigated by the police of Montgomery, Alabama. Some examples of police mistreatment were included in the ad, but later it was admitted that the description of this "terror" contained various errors.

On seeing this ad, L. B. Sullivan, a Montgomery city commissioner who supervised the police department, brought libel action against the *Times* and four black clergymen who had signed the ad. Although Sullivan was not named in the ad, he claimed that its publication defamed him because he was responsible for any actions that had been attributed to the Montgomery police. The trial jury awarded Sullivan $500,000 in damages, and this award was approved by the Alabama Supreme Court.

When the *Times* appealed the case to the United States Supreme Court, its lawyers argued that the newspaper assumed the sixty-four prominent persons who endorsed the ad would not have done so if they had known it contained some falsehoods. The *Times,* therefore, saw no reason to check the accuracy of the charges leveled against the Montgomery police. Furthermore, the paper took the position that freedom of the press protected by the First and Fourteenth Amendments justified its right to print the ad.

The Supreme Court unanimously reversed the decisions of the lower courts. The opening sentence of the Court opinion written by Justice William J. Brennan, Jr., confirmed that the justices had established an important rule for libel cases pertaining to public officials: "We are required in this case to determine for the first time the extent to which the constitutional protections for speech and press limit a State's powers to award damages in a libel action brought by a public official against critics of his official conduct." Brennan said that "the Constitutional guarantees require . . . a federal rule that prohibits a public official from recovering damages for a defamatory falsehood relating to his official conduct unless he proves that the statement was made with 'actual malice'—that is, with knowledge that it was false or with reckless disregard of whether it was false or not."

Thus, in one major ruling the Supreme Court decreed that it would be much more difficult for public officials than for private citizens to win libel suits. Private citizens could win their cases merely by proving that the media had been negligent in defaming them; public officials had to prove that the defamation sprang from deliberate malice.

In *New York Times Co. v. Sullivan,* the Court acknowledged that there were factual errors in the ad that the paper ran. But, as Brennan pointed out, it must be assumed that "erroneous statement is inevitable in free debate, and that it must be protected if the freedoms of expression are to have the 'breathing space' that they need . . . to survive."

In two 1967 cases the Supreme Court extended the proof-of-malice rule to "public figures" as well as public officials. This meant that people who were well known to the public also had to show that actual malice was intended in order to win libel suits.

Nearly twenty years later, in 1986, the Court again expanded the constitutional defense against libel suits. The case arose after the *Philadelphia Inquirer* published a series of articles seeking to link business executive Maurice S. Hepps to persons in organized crime. Hepps filed a libel suit against the paper, and when the Pennsylvania Supreme Court reviewed the case, it ruled that the newspaper had to prove that Hepps's charges were untrue.

However, the United States Supreme Court voted 5 to 4 to overturn this decision by the state court. It asserted that on matters of public concern, private individuals, like public figures, must be required to prove that any damaging statements by the media are false. Justice Sandra Day O'Connor, writing for the majority, explained that placing the burden of proof on media defendants could muzzle free speech by news organizations fearful of lawsuits.

The four dissenters, on the other hand, were concerned that this ruling could be a "blueprint for character assassination" and was contrary to society's strong interest in protecting innocent people from damaging statements that could hurt their reputations. Justice John Paul Stevens, joined by Chief Justice Warren E. Burger and Justices Byron R. White and William H. Rehnquist, declared: "I simply do not understand . . . why a character assassin should be given an absolute license to defame by means of statements that can be neither verified nor disproven."

Once again the Supreme Court had been confronted by a clash between two legitimate concerns of the American people—protecting a free press versus protecting individuals against libelous accusations—and, by a narrow one-vote margin, it decided which concern had the higher priority.

In 1988, the Supreme Court was faced with a different type of libel case—one that involved an outrageous satirical attack aimed at a public figure. In 1983 *Hustler,* the sexually explicit magazine, published a parody of a liquor ad in which it falsely portrayed the Rev. Jerry Falwell, former head of the Moral Majority, as a drunkard whose first sexual experience was with his mother in an outhouse.

Falwell sued for libel, but a jury rejected his claim, declaring that no reasonable person would believe the *Hustler* spoof was true. However, Falwell's suit also charged that the vicious cartoon caused him great emotional distress, and the jury agreed, awarding him $200,000 in damages. The jury's award to Falwell triggered anxiety among political cartoonists, satirists, comedians—anyone who might poke fun at public figures. But, in 1986, the 4th Circuit Court of Appeals upheld the lower court's decision.

After the Supreme Court reviewed the case, it rendered a unanimous verdict that public figures who are the victims of satire—even when it is outrageous and pornographic—may not sue for damages; it overturned the $200,000 judgment won by Falwell. Chief Justice William H. Rehnquist, writing for the Court, pointed to the nation's long tradition of permitting critics to lampoon politicians in print and in speech without fear of legal reprisals. Rehnquist explained that the Court did not want to create "an exception to the general First Amendment principles" by trying to draw a line between fair and unfair parodies of public figures. Also, he said, "Outrageousness in the area of political and social discourse has an inherent subjectiveness about it which would allow a jury to impose liability on the basis of jurors' tastes or views, or perhaps on the basis of their dislike of a particular expression."

Seven

FREEDOM of ASSOCIATION and ASSEMBLY

Congress shall make no law . . . abridging . . . the right of the people peaceably to assemble.

The First Amendment protects the right of the people to meet together and share ideas. Consider how important this right is. It permits us to join school clubs, church and synagogue groups, service organizations like the Scouts and the Peace Corps, labor unions and businesses, political parties, and groups formed to protest a specific action or policy.

Alexis de Tocqueville, a Frenchman who visited the United States in the 1830s, was very impressed by how many Americans joined together in various organizations. He wrote that ''Americans of all ages, all stations of life, and all types of dispositions are forever forming associations.''

He went on to observe that Americans joined together in groups whenever they wanted to hold a celebration, build a school, start a church, or do almost anything else. ''Finally,'' de Tocqueville said, ''if they want to proclaim a truth or propagate some feeling . . . they form an association. In every case, at the head of any new undertaking, where in France you would find the government . . . in the United States you are sure to find an association.''[1]

Most Americans take for granted their right of association. But, as de Tocqueville pointed out, in undemocratic societies, meetings are rigidly controlled by the government, lest the people might use such gatherings to air their grievances and possibly plot a rebellion. Throughout history, kings and dictators have known they may be able to stay in power if they can keep the people apart, since no rebellion can succeed if each individual has to act alone.

The freedom of association, however, is not absolute, even in a democracy. Restrictions of meetings are sometimes necessary to protect public safety or the security of the nation. The courts must be constantly vigilant to strike a fair balance between individual rights to assemble and the need to protect society.

The Supreme Court had to weigh these two factors in deciding the 1937 landmark case, *DeJonge* v. *Oregon.* Dirk DeJonge, a Communist, spoke at a party meeting in Portland, Oregon, that was called to protest alleged brutality by the local police. Even though the meeting was peaceful and DeJonge proposed no violent action, his membership in the Communist party and his participation at the meeting were considered sufficient grounds for arresting him. DeJonge was convicted and sentenced to seven years in prison for violating the local law that made it a crime to advocate "physical violence, sabotage, or any unlawful acts or methods as a means of accomplishing industrial change or political revolution."

The Supreme Court unanimously reversed DeJonge's conviction. Chief Justice Charles Evans Hughes declared that, consistent with the Constitution,

> . . . peaceable assembly for lawful discussion cannot be made a crime. The holding of meetings for peaceful political action cannot be proscribed [prohibited]. Those who assist in the conduct of such meetings cannot be branded as criminals on that score.

Two years later, another major case involving the freedom to assemble reached the High Court. The Committee for Industrial Organization (C.I.O.) sought a permit to use the parks and streets of Jersey City, New Jersey, for meetings in which its leaders would try to encourage workers to join their union. However, Frank Hague, the mayor of Jersey City, was opposed to the union movement and ordered that the C.I.O. be denied a permit to meet on the city's public property. The basis for his action was a city law that allowed officials to turn down requests for permits if they believed that "riot, disturbances, or disorderly meetings" could occur.

The C.I.O. then turned to the courts to prevent Mayor Hague from enforcing this law. When the case was appealed, the Supreme Court voted 5 to 2 to strike down the Jersey City permit law. Several justices wrote opinions upholding the C.I.O.'s use of public streets and parks. Justice Owen J. Roberts said, "Such use of the streets and parks has, from ancient times, been a part of the privileges, immunities, rights, and liberties of citizens." Roberts went on to explain that such rights are "not absolute, but relative, and must be exercised [in compliance] with peace and good order."

The Supreme Court did not oppose community restrictions on the freedom of assembly if such restrictions were reasonable and not used to silence people who had unpopular views. In the case of *Cox* v. *New Hampshire* (1941), the Court ruled unanimously that the officials of a New Hampshire town had acted constitutionally when they enforced a local law forbidding any parade or procession upon a public street unless a license had been obtained.

There were many civil rights demonstrations in the 1960s, and the courts often had to decide whether protest meetings conducted on public property were protected by the First Amendment. The most famous of these cases was *Edwards* v. *South Carolina*. On March 2, 1961, 187 black high school and college students in Columbia, South Car-

The 1960s saw a proliferation of civil rights demonstrations. In this march on Washington in 1963, many prominent civil rights leaders participated, including A. Philip Randolph, Roy Wilkins, and Martin Luther King, Jr.

olina, held a mass demonstration to protest racial discrimination. In groups of fifteen they marched from a nearby church to the statehouse, carrying signs that read "I am proud to be a Negro" and "Down with segregation." After the blacks had been marching for about forty-five minutes, the police ordered them to disperse within fifteen minutes or face arrest. They refused and remained on the grounds, giving speeches and singing patriotic and religious songs. The demonstrators were then arrested and charged with breach of the peace. They were convicted and ordered to pay fines or go to jail.

When this case reached the Supreme Court in 1963, the justices voted 8 to 1 in favor of the demonstrators. Justice Potter Stewart's opinion for the majority criticized South Carolina for enforcing a breach of the peace law that was worded much too broadly and vaguely. "And it is clear to us," Stewart wrote, "that in arresting, convicting, and punishing the [demonstrators] . . . South Carolina infringed [the demonstrators'] constitutionally protected rights of free speech, free assembly, and freedom to petition for redress of their grievances."

In 1987, the High Court heard an important case pertaining to women's rights. In Duarte, California, the local Rotary Club had admitted women to what had been an all-male organization. The Duarte chapter was then expelled by Rotary International, which carried its fight to exclude women to the courts.

A California law bans discrimination based on sex, and on this ground the state appeals court ruled in favor of the Duarte chapter. But then lawyers for Rotary International argued before the Supreme Court that California's anti-discrimination law is unconstitutional because it violates members' First Amendment guarantee to associate with whom they please. The Court had to decide between two cherished rights—freedom of association and equal opportunity for all Americans.

The justices voted unanimously to uphold the right of women to join the Rotary Club. Justice Lewis F. Powell, Jr., declared that Rotary International "failed to demonstrate that admitting women" would hamper the organization's ability to meet its goals. He added that even if the California law "does work some slight infringement on Rotary members' right of . . . association, that infringement is justified because it serves the state's compelling interest in eliminating discrimination against women."

In 1988, the Supreme Court took another important step toward ending discrimination in the membership of large private clubs. The case stemmed from a 1984 New York City public accommodations law, which said that clubs with more than 400 members that regularly serve meals and obtain part of their revenues by renting facilities to nonmembers were not truly private social groups and therefore had no right to restrict membership by sex, race, or religion. Other cities—including Los Angeles, Boston, Chicago, Washington, and San Francisco—had laws similar to the New York City ordinance.

The New York State Club Association, representing about 125 clubs, challenged the law on the grounds that it violated club members' constitutional rights to "freedom of association and privacy." Both rights have been implied to exist as part of the First Amendment's guarantees of freedom of speech and the right of the people peaceably to assemble.

When the case reached the Supreme Court, the justices agreed unanimously to uphold the New York City law, rejecting the notion that the Constitution gives clubs an absolute right to exclude whomever they choose. "It may well be that a considerable amount of private or intimate association occurs in such a [club] setting, as is also true in many restaurants and other places of accommodation," Justice Byron R. White wrote for the Court. "But that fact alone does not afford the entity as a whole any constitutional immunity to practice discrimination."

*Philip H. Lindsey, general secretary of
Rotary International, talks to reporters about the
Supreme Court's decision to uphold the right of
women to join the Rotary Club. The association
said they would abide by the Court's decision.*

LOYALTY OATHS

The right of association has never been more seriously challenged than during the Cold War years of the 1950s when millions of Americans believed that our national security was endangered by Communist subversion. Fear about Communist infiltration of labor unions led Congress to include in the 1947 Taft-Hartley Act a provision requiring all union officers to file a sworn statement that they were not members of, nor affiliated with, the Communist party and that they did not belong to any group believing in the forcible overthrow of the national government.

Union officials charged in court that this part of the Taft-Hartley Act was unconstitutional because it violated their right of association, but the Supreme Court, by a 5 to 1 vote in 1950, disagreed. The Court maintained that Congress could properly impose this regulation on union officers because of its power to prevent political strikes obstructing interstate commerce. Writing for the majority, Chief Justice Fred M. Vinson explained, "Congress could rationally find that the Communist party is not like other political parties in its utilization of positions of union membership as means by which to bring about strikes and other obstructions of commerce for purposes of political advantage."

The Supreme Court upheld loyalty tests in a series of cases in the 1950s. In *Adler* v. *Board of Education* (1952), it sustained a New York law stating that public employees could be dismissed if they belonged to any group included on a state list of "subversive" organizations. The Court agreed with a Maryland law requiring all candidates for public office to file sworn statements that they were never involved in any movement to violently overthrow the government. It also approved a Los Angeles loyalty oath for all city employees.

As the 1950s gave way to the 1960s, the High Court took a much more lenient position on punishing persons for their political affiliations. An Arizona loyalty oath was declared unconstitutional by a 5 to 4 vote in 1966, because it violated the First Amendment right of freedom of association by penalizing persons for membership in a suspect group regardless of whether they joined the group with the specific intention of committing unlawful acts.

A case that made the headlines in 1967 involved a challenge to the earlier *Adler* decision and to the loyalty oath imposed on teachers in New York. Every teacher in the state's public schools, including colleges and universities, had to sign a certificate saying that he or she was not a member of the Communist party or of any organization that the New York school system had listed as subversive. Any teacher belonging to one of these groups would be fired and would not be eligible to hold a job in any of the state's public schools. Four faculty members at the University of Buffalo refused to sign the certificates. After receiving their dismissal notices, they filed suit in federal district court, contending that their First Amendment rights had been denied.

In *Keyishian v. Board of Regents,* the Supreme Court, by a close vote of 5 to 4, reversed the *Adler* ruling and struck down the New York loyalty oath as unconstitutional. Said Justice William J. Brennan, Jr., writing for the majority:

> Our nation is deeply committed to safeguarding academic freedom, which is of transcendent value to all of us and not merely to the teachers concerned. That freedom is therefore a special concern of the First Amendment, which does not tolerate laws that cast a pall of orthodoxy over the classroom. The vigilant protection of constitutional freedoms is nowhere more vital than in the community of American schools.

Justice Tom C. Clark, speaking for the minority, said that the Court majority has "swept away one of our most precious rights, the right of self-preservation. . . ." Clark asserted that the minds of youth are developed in schools and that students should not be taught by anyone who ". . . is found to willfully and deliberately advocate, advise, or teach that our Government should be overthrown by force or violence . . ." or who "becomes a member of an organization that advocates such doctrine."

Eight

PROTECTION against SEARCH and SEIZURE

The right of the people to be secure in their persons, houses, papers, and effects, against unreasonable searches and seizures, shall not be violated, and no Warrants shall issue, but upon probable cause, supported by Oath or affirmation, and particularly describing the place to be searched, and the persons or things to be seized.

To ensure the safety of every community, the police have the responsibility to gather evidence of a crime and to arrest persons suspected of committing a crime. On the other hand, police should not be permitted to conduct reckless raids in which they ransack a person's home or business and carry back to the station anything they happen to find. Nor should police be allowed to seize a person unless they feel quite confident that this individual broke the law.

The Fourth Amendment protects people against *unreasonable* searches and seizures. In most situations, the police must have a valid warrant to carry on a search or make an arrest. This warrant must be obtained from a court magistrate or judge who has "probable cause" to believe that a law has been violated. And a search warrant must specify only that evidence which the police are seeking.

In 1914, the Supreme Court established an important rule about evidence in the case of *Weeks* v. *United States.* Fremont Weeks was convicted in a federal court of using the mails to promote an illegal lottery. The evidence used against him had been obtained, without a search warrant, when police got a key to his home, broke in, and seized documents and letters. Weeks appealed his conviction, claiming that the police had violated his Fourth Amendment rights.

The Supreme Court unanimously decided in favor of Weeks on the ground that the evidence taken improperly from his home could not be used in court against him. In this decision, a precedent known as the *exclusionary rule* was established: evidence seized illegally must be excluded from a trial and cannot be used to convict a defendant in any federal court. This 1914 rule did not pertain at that time to evidence used in state courts; the *Weeks* decision was handed down many years before the Supreme Court decreed that the Bill of Rights protects defendants in state cases.

One of the most interesting search-and-seizure cases was *Rochin* v. *California* (1952). Antonio Rochin was suspected of being a drug user and a drug dealer. Without a search warrant, police broke into his home and noticed two capsules lying on a nightstand in his bedroom. An officer shouted to Rochin, "Whose stuff is this?" Rochin then grabbed the pills and quickly swallowed them.

The police immediately seized Rochin and beat him hard on the back, trying to cause him to vomit. When this did not work, they rushed him to a hospital and had his stomach pumped. The two capsules, filled with morphine, were recovered and used as court evidence to help convict him.

Rochin's conviction was overturned by a unanimous vote of the Supreme Court. Justice Felix Frankfurter denounced the police tactics in this case as "conduct that shocks the conscience, . . . methods too close to the rack and screw'' to be accepted by society.

In the 1961 landmark case of *Mapp* v. *Ohio,* the Supreme Court extended the exclusionary rule to evidence presented in state courts. Acting on a tip that illegal gambling equipment was being hidden in Cleveland, Ohio, by Dollree Mapp, the police burst into her home without a warrant. They searched the entire home without finding what they were looking for, but they did discover obscene books and pictures that were illegal under Ohio law. Mapp was tried and convicted for possessing obscene materials.

Her lawyers fought her conviction all the way to the Supreme Court. By a 6 to 3 vote, the Court overturned Mapp's conviction. Justice Tom C. Clark wrote the majority opinion, saying that the evidence against the defendant had been ''secured by official lawlessness in flagrant abuse'' of constitutional rights. The court held that ''all evidence obtained by searches and seizures in violation of the Constitution is, by that same authority, inadmissible in a state court.'' To allow it to be admissible would tend ''to destroy the entire system of constitutional restraints on which the liberties of the people rest.''

There are a few instances when police do not need a warrant to conduct a search or make an arrest. If an officer sees a crime being committed, he or she obviously cannot wait to obtain a warrant before trying to apprehend the suspect. Should the same rule apply to searching an automobile, since its driver can speed away before the police can get a warrant? Or should an automobile, which is the owner's personal property, be protected, like a person's home, against warrantless searches?

In 1925, when prohibition was in effect and the consumption, sale, and transportation of liquor were illegal, George Carroll's car was searched by federal agents who had no warrant. They found liquor in his car, and this was used as evidence when a jury convicted Carroll of violat-

Dollree Mapp won her case against the state of Ohio, a landmark decision ruling in favor of an individual's right over a state's when evidence has been illegally obtained.

ing the federal prohibition law. The Supreme Court upheld his conviction, ruling that federal agents could make warrantless searches of automobiles if they had a reasonable suspicion of illegal actions.

The Court reaffirmed this position in a 1949 case and again in 1982, when a defendant's car trunk had been searched and was found to contain heroin. In 1985, the Court extended warrantless searches to include motor homes. Writing for the majority, Chief Justice Warren E. Burger explained that a motor home is more like a car than a dwelling and people expect to have less privacy in a motor home because such a house-vehicle is capable of traveling on the open road.

One of the most controversial cases in the 1970s involved searching the offices of a university newspaper. It grew out of an unruly disturbance at the Stanford University Hospital. Protest demonstrators had barricaded themselves in the hospital administrative offices and refused to leave. When nine police officers tried to force their way through the barricades, they were attacked with clubs. All nine officers were injured.

The *Stanford Daily,* a student newspaper, published photos of the clash, and from these the police were able to identify two of the attackers. They suspected there might be negatives showing other rioters in the files kept by the newspaper. The police got a warrant to search the paper's offices. The warrant contained no accusation against the newspaper, and the search revealed only the photographs that had previously appeared.

The important question in this case was not whether the police could obtain the photographs, but how they tried to get them. They used a search warrant, but there is another legal way to obtain evidence. The police could have used a court order called a *subpoena,* which would have required the newspaper officials to turn over to the court the specified photographs.

The *Stanford Daily* sued the Palo Alto police, in the name of Police Chief James Zurcher, for violating its First and Fourth Amendment rights. Lawyers for the newspaper claimed that since no one in the newsrooms was a suspect in the crime, the police should have gotten a subpoena rather than a warrant in seeking the photographs. Attorneys for the police argued that to require a subpoena for searches of nonsuspects' property would create a risk that the evidence might be destroyed before the subpoena could be obtained.

A district court and an appeals court both supported the claims of the *Stanford Daily*. The Supreme Court, however, by a vote of 5 to 3, struck down the decisions of the lower courts and ruled that the use of a search warrant in this case was permissible. Writing for the majority in *Zurcher, Chief of Police of Palo Alto* v. *The Stanford Daily* (1978), Justice Byron R. White asserted that ". . . valid warrants may be issued to search *any* property, whether or not occupied by a third party, at which there is probable cause to believe that . . . evidence of a crime will be found."

One of the dissenters, Justice John Paul Stevens, expressed concern about the possible effects of the *Zurcher* decision. "Countless law abiding citizens," he wrote, ". . . may have documents in their possession that relate to an ongoing criminal investigation. The consequences of subjecting this large category of persons to unannounced police searches are extremely dangerous."

Another type of search for evidence can be conducted from airplanes and helicopters. The Supreme Court reached different conclusions in two recent cases pertaining to air searches. In the first case, police suspected that a man in Santa Clara, California, was growing marijuana in his backyard. Instead of getting a search warrant to inspect his property, the police chartered a plane and flew over his backyard at an altitude of about 1,000 feet. They spotted the marijuana and then arrested the owner of the property for illegally growing these plants. The defendant charged that this warrantless aerial surveillance violated his Fourth Amendment protection against unreasonable searches.

When this case was heard by the Supreme Court in 1986, the justices voted 5 to 4 to uphold the conviction of the defendant. Chief Justice Warren E. Burger, writing for the majority, said, "In an age where private and commercial flight in the airways is routine, it is unreasonable for [the defendant] to expect that his marijuana plants were constitutionally protected from being observed with the naked eye from an altitude of 1,000 feet."

In dissent, Justice Lewis F. Powell, Jr., rejected Burger's comparison of the police air search with what would be seen on regularly scheduled commercial flights. He maintained that there is little chance that airplane passengers would be able or willing to observe and report on criminal activities from the sky. "Aerial surveillance is nearly as intrusive on family privacy as physical trespass . . ." Powell wrote. "It would appear that, after today, families can expect to be free of official surveillance only when they retreat behind the walls of their homes."

In 1987, when the Supreme Court ruled on a quite similar case, it seemed to contradict the decision it had made the previous year. This case arose because a police officer, flying on a helicopter patrol at an altitude of about 400 feet, noticed marijuana growing in a greenhouse in La Mesa, California. After getting a search warrant, a county sheriff went to the home, confiscated the plants, and arrested a person living there.

The Supreme Court voted 7 to 2 in favor of the defendant and upheld a state court order declaring low-altitude hovering a violation of the Fourth Amendment. The Court appeared to be saying in its 1986 and 1987 decisions that aerial surveillance is legal at an altitude of 1,000 feet but illegal at an altitude of 400 feet. This interpretation left law enforcement officers puzzled over exactly how low they can fly without crossing the legal line.

The search for drugs was the issue that led to two important Supreme Court decisions in 1988. One case arose in 1983 when federal narcotics agents spotted two men driving from a warehouse in trucks that later were found to be carrying marijuana. Instead of first obtaining a warrant to search the warehouse, the agents broke down its doors and discovered more marijuana. Then they went to a judge and got a warrant to search the warehouse and seize the marijuana.

The drug dealers were found guilty in the lower courts and appealed to the Supreme Court that their convictions should be reversed because the federal agents first searched their warehouse without a warrant. The justices conceded that the first search had been illegal, but, by a 4 to 3 vote, upheld the drug dealers' convictions. They concluded that if the agents had enough evidence to justify getting a warrant, this evidence should not have been excluded from the trial simply because it was found before the warrant was secured. Writing the majority opinion, Justice Antonin Scalia said, "While the government should not profit from its illegal activity, neither should it be placed in a worse position than it would otherwise have occupied."

In dissent, Justice Thurgood Marshall declared that this Court ruling "encourages illegal searches." He maintained that a dangerous precedent is established when "the police know in advance that they have little to lose and much to gain by forgoing the bother of obtaining a warrant and undertaking an illegal search."

The other 1988 Supreme Court decision involving a drug search answered this question: Can the police, without a warrant, search garbage that has been left at curbside in front of a person's house? The case stemmed from a 1984 police investigation in Laguna Hills, California. Acting on a tip that Billy Greenwood was a drug dealer, the police asked the local refuse collector to give them the brown plastic trash bags left in front of Greenwood's house. Inside the bags officers found drug paraphernalia and a trace of cocaine. Using this evidence to obtain a search warrant, the police entered Greenwood's house and discovered several pounds of cocaine and some hashish.

Greenwood protested the original warrantless search of his trash bags, claiming it violated the Fourth Amendment ban on unreasonable searches and seizures. The California Supreme Court had decreed in 1971 that searches of discarded trash were unconstitutional, so state courts were obliged to follow that rule.

The United States Supreme Court, however, overturned the decision of the California courts. By a 6 to 2 vote, the justices ruled that incriminating evidence obtained from garbage without a warrant could be used against Greenwood. According to Justice Byron R. White, writing for the majority, the search was valid because Greenwood could have no "reasonable" expectation of privacy in his garbage. "It is common knowledge," White asserted, "that plastic garbage bags left on or at the side of a public street are readily accessible to animals, children, scavengers, snoops, and other members of the public. . . . What a person knowingly exposes to the public is not a subject of Fourth Amendment protection."

Justice William J. Brennan, Jr., writing the minority opinion, viewed the case differently. "A single bag of trash testifies eloquently to the eating, reading, and recreational habits of the person who produced it," he said. "Scrutiny of another's trash is contrary to commonly accepted notions of civilized behavior."

Other aspects of searches and seizures will be discussed in Chapter 10, which deals with the right of privacy.

Nine

RIGHTS of the ACCUSED

In the United States a person suspected of committing a crime is considered innocent unless and until proven guilty. The Bill of Rights provides constitutional safeguards to protect the rights of individuals charged with breaking the law. Amendments Five and Six are intended to guarantee that accused persons will be treated fairly and justly by the officers who arrest them and by the courts where their cases will be tried. Amendment Eight protects those who are arrested from excessive, or unreasonable, bail. It also protects those who have been convicted of crimes from punishments that are cruel and unusual.

A FAIR AND SPEEDY TRIAL

In all criminal prosecutions, the accused shall enjoy the right to a speedy and public trial, by an impartial jury of the State and district wherein the crime shall have been committed.

The system of trials by jury is deeply rooted in English history. Jury trials were being conducted in England three centuries before the first English settlers arrived in the New World. Americans were determined that the Bill of Rights would include the guarantee of a public, speedy trial for anyone charged with committing a crime.

In federal criminal cases these three rules pertaining to jury trials have been consistently followed: (1) the jury is composed of twelve members, (2) the trial is supervised by a judge who has the authority to instruct the jurors, and (3) the jury's verdict must be unanimous.

The same rules have not always been followed in criminal cases tried in state courts. In fact, states were not required to provide the accused a jury trial in criminal prosecutions until the Supreme Court ruled in a 1968 case that jury trials were guaranteed by the Sixth and Fourteenth Amendments. Two differences between juries in federal courts and juries in state courts are that in state criminal trials juries may be composed of as few as six members and twelve-member juries do not have to reach a unanimous verdict.

In 1972, the Supreme Court heard two criminal cases in which twelve-member juries in state courts had not reached a unanimous verdict. The High Court allowed these verdicts to stand. But, in a 1979 case, the justices ruled that a state deprives a defendant of constitutional rights if it allows that person to be convicted by a non-unanimous vote of a six-member jury.

Juries are supposed to consist of persons from every walk of life who represent a wide variety of groups in the community. However, for many years blacks were not selected for jury duty in parts of the South. The Supreme Court finally dealt with this form of racial discrimination in a 1935 case. Clarence Norris, a black, had been accused of raping a white woman and convicted by a jury made up entirely of white persons. He then charged that his Sixth Amendment right to an impartial jury trial and his Fourteenth Amendment right to equal protection of the laws had been denied. Evidence was shown that even though many blacks lived in the community, none had ever been called for jury duty. Reasoning that blacks in this area had

*Clarence Norris, forty-one years after the
Supreme Court reversed his conviction by an all-white
jury, thus supporting his right to an impartial jury*

been intentionally excluded from juries, the Supreme Court voted unanimously to reverse the conviction of Norris.

Thirteen years later the Court reviewed a somewhat similar case in which a black man had been convicted of murder by an all-white jury and sentenced to death by electrocution. Again, the justices voted unanimously to overturn the man's conviction. Chief Justice Charles Evans Hughes explained this decision in *Patton* v. *Mississippi* (1948), saying that when a jury plan always results in the exclusion of all blacks, indictments reached by such juries cannot stand. However, Hughes added, this "does not mean that a guilty defendant must go free. For indictments can be returned and convictions can be obtained by juries selected as the Constitution commands."

In some communities women were exempted from jury duty. As recently as the early 1960s, seventeen states made jury service voluntary for women. In Florida, Gwendolyn Hoyt, who was charged with murdering her husband with a baseball bat, contended that she had not received a fair trial before an all-male jury because the state excluded women from mandatory jury duty. The Supreme Court, which heard the case of *Hoyt* v. *Florida* in 1961, unanimously sustained the Florida law, saying that it did not exclude female jurors but let women decide whether they wanted to serve in the jury box. The Court rationalized its sexist decision on the ground that the state had an interest in preventing interference with women's traditional functions as wives, mothers, and homemakers.

The feminist movement had gathered momentum by 1975 when the Supreme Court voted 8 to 1 to overturn the *Hoyt* decision. In the case of *Taylor* v. *Louisiana,* the Court decreed that state laws that exempted women from jury duty violated the defendant's Sixth Amendment promise of a fair, impartial trial before jurors drawn from a wide cross-section of people in the community.

In a 1967 case, the Supreme Court asserted that the right to a speedy trial is "as fundamental as any of the rights secured by the Sixth Amendment." At that time the Court overturned a North Carolina law which permitted criminal trials to be postponed for long periods of time. But court schedules often are crowded with many pending trials, and it is sometimes difficult to determine whether the delay of a trial is reasonable or unreasonable.

The Supreme Court had to rule on the "speedy trial" issue in a 1986 case. Four men had been arrested by Oregon police in 1975 for illegally transporting time bombs, dynamite, guns, and ammunition. The trial was delayed for years as the prosecution and the defense argued about whether the charges could be dismissed and what evidence would be allowed in the courtroom. Finally, in 1983, a district court decided that the defendants' rights to a speedy trial had been violated and dismissed the charges against them. The U.S. Ninth Circuit Court of Appeals upheld this ruling.

But the Supreme Court did not agree with the decisions made by the lower courts. By a 5 to 4 vote, the justices ruled that the defendants could be tried eleven years after they were first arrested and charged with illegally transporting firearms and explosives. Justice Lewis F. Powell, Jr., writing for the majority, declared: "There is no showing of bad faith or dilatory [stalling] purpose on the government's part. The government's position in each of the appeals was strong."

The four dissenters believed that this trial's lengthy delay was inexcusable. One of them, Justice Thurgood Marshall, wrote that "the government—not the defendants—should suffer from the consequences of delays. . . ."

ASSISTANCE OF COUNSEL

In all criminal prosecutions, the accused shall enjoy the right . . . to have the Assistance of Counsel for his defense.

Law is a very complex subject, and the average person needs the assistance of counsel (an attorney) in most lawsuits. But what if the defendant is too poor to hire an attorney? Can that person have equal treatment under the law if he or she is involved in a trial without the aid of a trained, experienced member of the legal profession?

In the 1938 case of *Johnson* v. *Zerbst,* the Supreme Court made it clear that the defendant must be provided an attorney in all criminal cases held in federal courts. If the defendant cannot afford an attorney, then the government must pay for one. But this ruling said nothing about requiring defense attorneys in criminal cases in state courts. In fact, in a 1942 case *(Betts* v. *Brady),* the Court declared that states did not have to supply counsel to defendants too poor to employ an attorney.

This was the situation when Clarence Earl Gideon was arrested by Florida police for breaking into a poolroom and smashing a cigarette machine and jukebox to get money. Unable to afford a lawyer, Gideon asked the court to appoint one to act in his defense. The judge denied his request, explaining that under Florida law the only time the court can appoint an attorney is when the defendant is charged with a crime involving the death penalty.

Gideon was convicted and sentenced to five years in prison. While in prison, he carefully prepared his own petitions, asking higher courts to overturn his conviction because he had been refused his constitutional right to counsel. When his case reached the Supreme Court in 1963, the Court appointed a highly respected lawyer, Abe Fortas, to argue in Gideon's behalf.

The Supreme Court voted unanimously to reverse Gideon's conviction and overturn its earlier *Betts* ruling. Justice Hugo L. Black wrote the opinion, saying that the right-to-counsel provision of the Sixth Amendment is "fundamental and essential to a fair trial" in both federal and state courts.

The next year, the High Court heard another landmark case, *Escobedo* v. *Illinois* (1964), pertaining to right

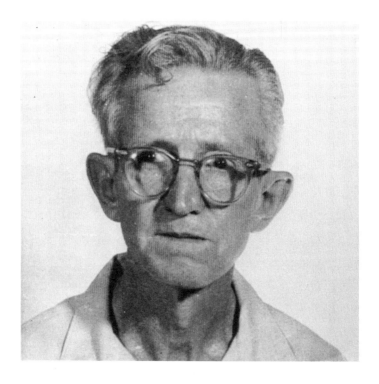

*After his first appeal was denied,
Clarence Earl Gideon won his appeal to
the Supreme Court. What is referred to
as the Gideon Decision guarantees all
defendants free counsel when charged
with a major crime. Immediately after
the Supreme Court's decision, 4,000
Florida convicts sought new trials.*

to counsel. Danny Escobedo had been arrested for murder
in Illinois. During his police interrogation, he repeatedly
asked for the aid of his attorney, but this request was denied. Also, he was not told that he had the right to remain
silent and not answer any questions during his interrogation. When Escobedo's trial began, some of the statements
he had made earlier when the police questioned him were

used against him, and he was found guilty. Escobedo challenged the verdict, contending that because his right to counsel and his right to remain silent had been violated, he had not received a fair and impartial trial.

The Supreme Court wrestled with this difficult case, and, by a narrow vote of 5 to 4, struck down Escobedo's conviction. Writing for the majority, Justice Arthur J. Goldberg said:

> We have . . . learned . . . that no system of criminal justice can, or should, survive if it comes to depend for its continued effectiveness on the citizens' abdication through unawareness of their constitutional rights. No system worth preserving should have to *fear* that if an accused is permitted to consult with a lawyer, he will become aware of, and exercise, these rights. If the exercise of constitutional rights will thwart the effectiveness of a system of law enforcement, then there is something very wrong with that system.

Justice Byron R. White wrote a strongly worded minority opinion that was highly critical of the decision reached by the majority. "The right to counsel," White declared, "now not only entitles the accused to counsel's advice and aid in preparing for trial, but stands as an impenetrable barrier to any interrogation once the accused has become a suspect."

SELF-INCRIMINATION

No person . . . shall be compelled in any criminal case to be a witness against himself.

You may have read or heard that someone suspected of a crime "took the Fifth Amendment." This means that the suspect exercised his or her constitutional right not to say anything that might be incriminating. The protection against self-incrimination, which has been observed by

Danny Escobedo (right) and his attorney during his trial on burglary charges, two years after his landmark case. In that case he was freed of murder charges after the Supreme Court found his constitutional rights violated.

federal authorities since the early days of our republic, was extended to the states by a 1964 Supreme Court decision (*Malloy* v. *Hogan, Sheriff*).

The most famous case involving self-incrimination was *Miranda* v. *Arizona,* which the High Court acted upon in 1966. Ernesto Miranda was arrested for the kidnapping and rape of an eighteen-year-old girl in Arizona. He was questioned by the police for two hours, and then he signed a confession. Statements Miranda made after his arrest and the confession he signed during police interrogation were used against him at his trial. He was found guilty and sentenced to prison for twenty to thirty years.

Miranda, however, claimed that the evidence used against him had been illegally obtained. He said that before the police questioned him they had not advised him of his Fifth Amendment right to remain silent and his Sixth Amendment right to counsel. While Miranda was in prison, his lawyer appealed the case, and eventually it reached the Supreme Court. The justices voted 5 to 4 in favor of Miranda.

Chief Justice Earl Warren, writing for the majority, declared that this case raised "questions which go to the roots of our concepts of American criminal jurisprudence." These questions, he continued, involved "the constraints society must observe consistent with the federal Constitution in prosecuting individuals for crime."

Warren said the police must observe three rules to assure the defendant of his or her constitutional rights. First, "At the outset, if a person in custody is to be subjected to interrogation, he must be informed in clear and unequivocal [certain] terms that he has the right to remain silent." Second, "The warning of the right to remain silent must be accompanied by the explanation that anything said can and will be used against the individual in court." Third, the suspect must be told that he has the right to the presence of an attorney during his interrogation and "if he is indigent a lawyer will be appointed to represent him."

The four dissenting justices were disturbed about the far-reaching implications of the *Miranda* decision. Justice Byron R. White wrote, "There is, in my view, every reason to believe that a good many criminal defendants who otherwise would have been convicted . . . will now, under this new version of the Fifth Amendment, either not be tried at all or will be acquitted if the State's evidence, minus the confession, is put to the test of litigation."

Justice John Marshall Harlan echoed White's concern when he declared that the Court "is taking a real risk with society's welfare in imposing its new rules" for police procedure in dealing with suspects. "The social costs of crime are too great to call the new rules anything but a hazardous experimentation."

Few Court decisions have aroused so much controversy throughout the country, and the argument about the *Miranda* rules still continues. On the one side are those who defend the rules as necessary to protect the rights of the accused. On the other side are those who claim that *Miranda* "coddles criminals" and makes the task of law enforcement much more difficult.

Various steps have been taken by Congress and the Supreme Court to "water down" or blunt the effect of *Miranda*. In 1968, Congress passed the Crime Control and Safe Streets Act, which says that confessions can be used in federal trials whenever the judge rules that they are voluntary. Three years later, the Supreme Court decreed that voluntary statements made by a defendant not warned of his or her rights may still be used to question the suspect's truthfulness if that person takes the witness stand and contradicts earlier statements.

Several Supreme Court decisions in the 1980s have further weakened *Miranda* rules. In one case, the Court upheld the conviction of a Colorado man who confessed to a murder after hearing "voices from God." The justices ruled in this decision that *Miranda* was intended only to protect against "coercive political activity," not to assure that suspects are "totally rational" when they admit to crimes. Another case involved a man who was picked up by the police for carrying firearms, read his *Miranda* rights, and then questioned about something else—the murder of his hunting partner. Although the suspect had been deceived by the police, the Supreme Court upheld his conviction by a vote of 7 to 2. Justice Lewis F. Powell, Jr., writing the majority opinion, explained that the *Miranda* warnings specify that "anything he said could be used as evidence against him. The Constitution does not require that a suspect know and understand every possible consequence of a waiver of the Fifth Amendment privilege."

The Supreme Court created a major exception to the *Miranda* rules in a 1986 case when it decided that police do not need to advise suspects of their constitutional rights before taking necessary steps to protect public safety. Benjamin Quarles was chased into a New York City store by police who suspected that he had raped a young woman. While frisking the man, officers found an empty shoulder holster and asked where the weapon was. "The gun is over there," the suspect replied, pointing to a nearby carton. After seizing the gun, an officer read the man his *Miranda* rights.

The lower courts ruled that both the gun and Quarles's statement about it could not be used as evidence against him because police had failed to read him his rights beforehand. But the Supreme Court, by a 6 to 3 vote, overturned these earlier decisions, reasoning that as long as the gun was concealed, people nearby were in danger because it could have been used by an accomplice. "We conclude that the need for answers to questions in a situation posing a threat to the public safety outweighs the need for the . . . rule protecting the Fifth Amendment's privilege against self-incrimination," wrote Justice William H. Rehnquist for the majority.

CRUEL AND UNUSUAL PUNISHMENT

Excessive bail shall not be required, nor excessive fines imposed, nor cruel and unusual punishment inflicted.

In November 1944, a druggist in St. Martinville, Louisiana, was found shot to death near his home. The police were unable to find any clues to the murder. Then, by chance, a person named Willie Francis, who had lived in St. Martinville, was stopped in Texas for routine questioning. In Francis's pocket the police found the wallet of the murdered man. Willie Francis signed a confession that he had killed the druggist and was returned to St. Martinville, where he was tried, found guilty, and sentenced to die in the electric chair.

The execution was set for May 3, 1946, and precisely at noon Francis was strapped to the electric chair. Then the electrodes were attached to his body, the hood was placed over his head, and the switch was turned on. Francis groaned with pain, pulled against the straps, and jumped so hard that the chair came off the floor—but he did not die. The executioner turned off the switch and quickly turned it on again. But because of some mechanical defect, the small charge of electricity, which made Francis writhe in pain, was not sufficient to put him to death. He was unstrapped and taken back to his cell, and the sheriff announced that the execution would be postponed.

This bizarre incident made front-page news across the country, and pressure against a second electrocution attempt began to build. Francis's lawyer appealed to the Supreme Court, claiming that since his client had suffered from one painful shock of electricity, to send him to the electric chair again would violate his Eighth Amendment protection against cruel and unusual punishment. The lawyer also contended that Francis's execution would be a denial of the double jeopardy clause of the Fifth Amendment that prohibits double prosecution and double punishment for the same offense in criminal cases.

When this unusual case was heard by the Supreme Court in 1947, the justices had difficulty in reaching a decision. Finally, by a narrow 5 to 4 vote, the Court ruled that Francis could be sent to the electric chair a second time. (He was electrocuted a little more than a year after his first "execution day.") Writing the majority opinion, Justice Stanley F. Reed said, "The cruelty against which the Constitution protects a convicted man is cruelty inherent in the method of punishment, not the necessary suffering involved in any method employed to extinguish life humanely."

Justice Harold H. Burton, speaking for the minority, asserted, "When life is to be taken, there must be no avoidable error of law or uncertainty of fact." Burton asserted that "taking life by unnecessarily cruel means shocks the most fundamental instincts of civilized man."

The issue of capital punishment (putting a person to death for a crime) has sharply divided the American public. Many people believe that the death penalty is a proper punishment for individuals who commit the most serious crimes, and that executions serve as examples to forewarn other potential criminals not to endanger the public safety. Other Americans contend that capital punishment is a cruel and unacceptable practice in a humane society and that it does not prevent other crimes from occurring.

The Supreme Court, in 1972, reviewed the basic question of whether capital punishment should be permitted. It handed down similar decisions in three related cases: *Furman* v. *Georgia, Branch* v. *Texas,* and *Jackson* v. *Georgia.* By the same close vote of 5 to 4 in each case, the Court overturned all existing death penalty laws on the grounds that they violated the Eighth and Fourteenth Amendments.

Nine different opinions were written on these narrowly decided cases. Justices William J. Brennan, Jr., and Thurgood Marshall took the position that under no circumstances could the death penalty be tolerated in our democratic society. Brennan declared that capital punishment was "uniquely degrading to human dignity" and there was no substantial evidence to prove that it "serves any penal purpose more effectively than the less severe punishment of imprisonment."

The other three justices in the majority—William O. Douglas, Byron R. White, and Potter Stewart—based their opposition to the death penalty mainly on the inconsistent, unfair ways in which various states imposed this penalty. They were concerned because some convicted defendants were put to death while others were sent to prison for the same crimes. Justice Stewart pointed out that death sentences that were left entirely to the discretion of juries often resulted in "wanton and freakish" decisions.

These 1972 rulings ended capital punishment in all the states. But the High Court left the door open for the return of the death penalty if the states would rewrite their laws to conform to either of two new procedures. One procedure was to have the death penalty mandatory (required) for specific crimes, which would eliminate any unreasonable decision by a jury. The second procedure called for two stages in cases involving capital punishment. In the first stage, the guilt or innocence of the defendant would be determined. In the second stage, a separate hearing would be held to decide whether the circumstances leading to the crime warranted the death penalty.

Thirty-seven states adopted new death penalty laws, but the Supreme Court did not automatically accept all of them as constitutional. In 1976, it threw out laws in North Carolina and Louisiana that made the death penalty mandatory for all individuals convicted of first-degree murder. The Court ruled that these laws had been too narrowly drawn because they allowed no consideration for the defendant or for any special circumstances pertaining to the crime.

But on the same day that the justices struck down the mandatory death penalty laws of North Carolina and Louisiana, they approved, by a vote of 7 to 2, the two-stage procedure that had been established in three other states. In *Gregg* v. *Georgia* (1976), one of the three cases, the Court decreed that the punishment of death for the crime of murder does not, under all circumstances, violate the Eighth and Fourteenth Amendments.

Since 1976, the Court usually has upheld as constitutional the two-stage procedure adopted by many states. But it generally has overturned state laws requiring the death penalty for specific crimes because most of these laws have left no leeway for a less severe sentence when there were special circumstances pertaining to a criminal act. For example, the Court struck down a Georgia law that required the death penalty for rape and a Louisiana law that imposed a mandatory death sentence on defendants convicted of the first-degree murder of a police officer.

Three significant death penalty cases were heard by the Supreme Court in 1987. In one case, by a 5 to 4 vote, the Court extended the grounds for capital punishment to include an accomplice who plays a major role in a crime leading to murder, even if that participant did not intend that the victim be killed. The Court decided in another case, again by a 5 to 4 vote, that a jury deliberating the fate of a convicted killer may not be told about the impact of the crime on the victim's family. The justices ruled in this case that the court system must tilt in the direction of ensuring fairness for a defendant, even though this means excluding the anguished statements made by the victim's distraught relatives.

The third important 1987 case involved a black man who killed a white policeman in Atlanta, Georgia. Lawyers opposed to capital punishment presented evidence that killers of whites were more likely than killers of blacks to be sentenced to death in several Southern states. They cited a study that claimed murderers were eleven times more likely to receive the death sentence if the victim was white rather than black.

If the Court majority had concluded in this case that the death penalty was tainted with racism, it could have struck down all state capital punishment laws, as it did in 1972. However, by another 5 to 4 vote, the Court upheld the death penalty and rejected as inconclusive the statistical evidence presented by the defense. Justice Lewis F. Powell, Jr., speaking for the majority, conceded that Georgia's legal system might be unfair to blacks, but he insisted that statistics alone could not prove that "purposeful discrimination" was responsible for the death sentence imposed on the black killer of the white Atlanta policeman. In this particular case, Powell said, there was no evidence that jurors discriminated against the defendant because of race.

In dissent, Justice William J. Brennan, Jr., asserted that the "dual system of crime and punishment" which treated blacks and whites differently before the Civil War is "still effectively in place" in Georgia.

In 1988, the Supreme Court considered the case of a man who had been sentenced to death for a crime he commited at the age of fifteen. William Wayne Thompson participated with three other persons in the brutal murder of his sister's former husband in 1983. Oklahoma, where the crime occurred, is one of nineteen states that authorizes capital punishment without setting any minimum age. The other eighteen states that permit capital punishment do not allow execution for crimes committed under the age of sixteen.

The Supreme Court voted 5 to 3 to reverse Thompson's death sentence. Four members of the Court said in an opinion written by Justice John Paul Stevens that "evolving standards of decency" compelled the conclusion that it would be unconstitutional under any circumstances to execute a person for a crime committed at the age of fifteen. Justice Sandra Day O'Connor voted with the majority, but said that her conclusions were somewhat different from those of the other justices who agreed to spare Thompson's life. She wrote, "Although I believe that a national consensus forbidding the execution of any person for a crime committed before the age of sixteen very likely does exist, I am reluctant to adopt the conclusion as a matter of constitutional law without better evidence than we now possess."

Justice Antonin Scalia, one of the dissenters, declared that the Eighth Amendment's ban on cruel and unusual punishments was not originally intended to prohibit execution of juveniles. The Court's decision to strike down Thompson's death sentence, he said, "limits the evolving standards appropriate for our consideration to those entertained by society rather than those dictated by our personal consciences."

Ten

RIGHT to PRIVACY

There is not a single word about privacy in the Bill of Rights, yet this is one of our most cherished rights. As Supreme Court Justice Louis D. Brandeis said in 1928, "The right to be let alone [is] the most comprehensive of rights and the right most valued by civilized men."[1]

Without referring to the term "privacy," various constitutional amendments protect certain aspects of our right to be let alone. The privacy of opinions, beliefs, and associations is safeguarded by the First Amendment. The privacy of our homes against soldiers being quartered there is guaranteed by the Third Amendment. Our protection against unreasonable government intrusions is provided by the Fourth Amendment. The prohibition against self-incrimination in the Fifth Amendment guards our innermost secrets from invasion by the courts. And the Ninth Amendment says that we retain fundamental rights not expressly listed in the Constitution or its amendments.

Absolute privacy is impossible to attain, nor is it even desirable. Our society needs to have certain information about people in order to function effectively. Without such information, other important values, such as fairness, justice, and equality, could be obliterated. For example, internal revenue agents must know a person's income so that he or she can be assessed a fair and equitable income tax. Law enforcement officers need to find out if a person arrested for molesting a child has ever committed this crime before, so that the court can determine a just punishment and society can be better protected against repeated offenses. Government authorities must know if a person had been denied a job because of race or sex in order to enforce the laws against discrimination.

Today, in the age of high-tech computers, there is a new way to invade our privacy that was not available in the past. A large number of government agencies and private businesses are now using computerized data banks in which hundreds of facts about a person can be stored on a silicon chip no larger than the head of a pin. Some scientists predict that in the future one central computer will be able to keep detailed tabs on every human being in any country and to update this information every minute or so.

The collection and dissemination of such vast amounts of information raise some profound moral and legal questions. Should a computer be permitted to record and release to others intimate details about a person's medical history? Should computerized data determine whether an individual can get a bank loan? Should computer operators be allowed to find out the buying habits of consumers and then sell to companies the names of people who might be interested in their products? All of these computer uses violate the privacy of individuals.

There are other questions about the invasion of privacy which are not necessarily linked to computers. For instance, is it proper for owners of businesses who fear thefts inside their companies to subject their employees to periodic lie detection tests? In the interest of combating the serious drug abuse problem, should professional and college athletes be forced to have medical examinations that show whether they have been on drugs? To protect society against the spread of AIDS, should there be compulsory blood tests for certain classes of people, such as inmates in a federal prison, patients in a Veterans Administration hospital, immigrants seeking to reside in the United States, and couples applying for a marriage licence?

Some of these controversial questions that pit the right to privacy against the needs of society may eventually be heard by the Supreme Court.

EAVESDROPPING

The High Court has already dealt with the privacy question involved in eavesdropping, or listening in on someone's private conversation. The oldest and best known form of electronic eavesdropping is wiretapping a telephone line. Bugging is a more recent type of intercepting conversations. "Bugs," which usually consist of a tiny radio transmitter, microphone, and amplifier, can be placed in a telephone receiver to pick up conversations. Or they may be "planted" almost anywhere in a room. Today, there also are sophisticated eavesdropping devices that use laser beams to detect voice vibrations on a window of a room where people are talking.

In 1928, the Supreme Court was confronted with the wiretapping issue for the first time, in the case of *Olmstead* v. *United States*. This case involved a bootlegging conspiracy that operated during the era of Prohibition. The information that led to the exposure of the bootlegging ring was largely obtained by intercepting telephone messages. This wiretapping was done in the basement of the building that housed the bootleggers' offices.

When the warrantless conversations were used as evidence against the defendants in court, they charged that their Fourth Amendment protection against unlawful seizures had been violated. The Supreme Court, however, voted 5 to 4 to uphold their convictions. Chief Justice William Howard Taft, delivering the majority opinion, reasoned that only the spoken word had been seized, and the spoken word, he argued, was not protected by the Fourth Amendment.

In his famous dissent, Justice Louis D. Brandeis asked an important question: "Can it be that the Constitution affords no protection against such invasions of personal security?" To Brandeis, the answer was obvious. "Every unjustifiable intrusion upon the privacy of the individual, whatever the means employed, must be deemed a violation of the Fourth Amendment."

Despite the logic of Brandeis's argument, from 1928 until 1967 the Supreme Court ruled that the Fourth Amendment applied only when there was illegal entry or tangible items were seized. Listening in on a private conversation without a court warrant was not considered breaking the law.

As the years passed, new justices with different views were appointed to the Supreme Court. In 1967 the eavesdropping case that the justices heard involved the use of evidence that government agents obtained against Charles Katz, who was accused of illegal gambling activities. Most of the evidence came from a listening and recording device attached to the outside of a public telephone booth where Katz had secret conversations.

By a vote of 7 to 1, the Supreme Court reversed the *Olmstead* decision and decreed that warrantless eavesdropping violated the Fourth Amendment. Justice Potter Stewart, writing for the majority, said:

> . . . the Fourth Amendment protects people, not places. What a person knowingly exposes to the public, even in his own home or office, is not a subject of Fourth Amendment protection. . . . But what he seeks to preserve as private, even in an area accessible to the public, may be constitutionally protected. . . .
>
> What [Katz] sought to exclude when he entered the booth was not the intruding eye—it was

the uninvited ear. He did not shed his right to do so simply because he made his calls from a place where he might be seen.

The year after the *Katz* decision, Congress passed the Crime Control and Safe Streets Act that spelled out the rules for legal eavesdropping. A warrant to wiretap or bug someone's conversation must be obtained from a Justice Department official or a judge who has been convinced by the FBI or police that there is probable cause of criminal activity which may be detected by the electronic device.

MARRIAGE AND SEXUAL CONDUCT

Should the government have the authority to interfere with such intimate matters as whether a married couple want to have children?

Long ago, in 1879, Connecticut enacted a stringent law that made it a crime for anyone, including married persons, to use contraceptives. The law further provided that any person who assists, counsels, or causes another individual to use contraceptives could be prosecuted and punished.

Mrs. Estelle Griswold, the director of a birth control clinic in New Haven, Connecticut, was arrested and fined one hundred dollars for giving information and advice on birth control measures to married persons. Her conviction was upheld by an appellate court and by Connecticut's highest court. Then it was brought on appeal to the Supreme Court.

By a 7 to 2 vote in 1965, the Court reversed Griswold's conviction and struck down the Connecticut contraceptive law. Writing the majority opinion, Justice William O. Douglas asserted, "Would we allow the police to search the sacred precincts of marital bedrooms for telltale signs of the use of contraceptives? The very idea is repulsive to the notions of privacy surrounding the marriage relationship.''

Two years later, in 1967, the Court dealt with a Virginia law that made it a crime to have an interracial marriage. The justices overturned this law on the grounds that the freedom to marry a person of another race rests entirely with the individuals and cannot be interfered with by the state.

ABORTION

Few issues have divided the nation as sharply in recent years as abortion. Many Americans believe that the woman herself, not the government, should decide whether she wants to terminate her own pregnancy. Many other Americans believe that after a woman becomes pregnant and carries a live fetus, the willful destruction of this fetus is a form of murder.

On January 22, 1973, the Supreme Court handed down a landmark decision on abortion. Two similar cases, *Roe* v. *Wade* and *Doe* v. *Bolton,* came from Texas and Georgia, states that had stringent laws preventing women from having abortions except under extreme conditions. (''Roe'' and ''Doe'' were fictitious names used to protect the identities of the women who challenged the laws.)

By a 7 to 2 vote, the High Court struck down the Texas and Georgia abortion laws. Writing the majority opinion, Justice Harry A. Blackmun declared that the right to privacy ''is broad enough to encompass a woman's decision whether or not to terminate her pregnancy.'' However, Blackmun explained, this was not an absolute right, so the Court established certain regulations pertaining to the different stages of pregnancy.

In the first trimester (three months) of pregnancy, a

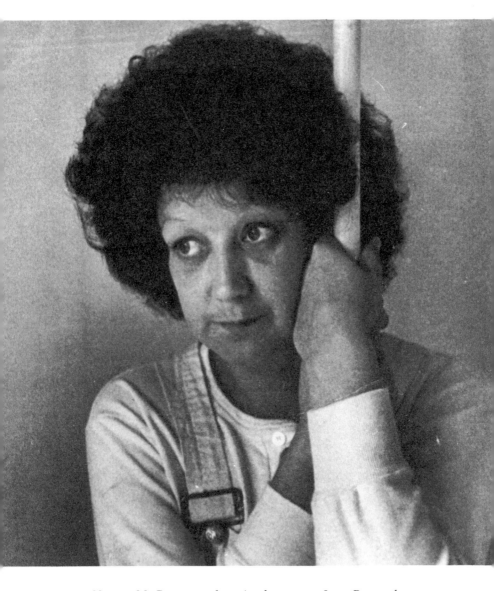

*Norma McCorvey, otherwise known as Jane Roe, whose
desire for an abortion triggered a landmark decision
in* Roe v. Wade, *poses for a photograph ten years after
the historic decision, which remains controversial.*

woman and her doctor may decide without any state interference whether she is to have an abortion. In the second trimester, a state may interfere with an abortion only when such an operation would be likely to harm the woman's health. During the final trimester, when the fetus could live on its own outside the body, the state's compelling interest is to protect the life of the fetus. Therefore, states can enact laws forbidding abortion in the last three months of pregnancy, except in cases where abortion is necessary to protect the woman's life or health.

The *Roe* decision did not end the argument over abortion; instead, it simply fanned the fire of controversy. Those who supported the Court ruling rejoiced that the justices had affirmed the rights of women to include the power to decide whether they wanted to give birth. The "pro-life" people who opposed the Court ruling vowed to continue the fight against abortion. They were encouraged when Ronald Reagan, an ardent anti-abortionist, became president in 1981. President Reagan advocated a constitutional amendment to overturn *Roe* and return the regulation of abortion to state control.

In 1980, the Supreme Court ruled that the states do not have to pay for abortions for poor women. But, in 1983, the justices struck down some of the restrictions on abortion, such as the requirements that abortions performed on women more than three months pregnant must take place in hospitals and that there must be a 24-hour waiting period before the operation is started.

The most important abortion case since *Roe* was heard by the Supreme Court in 1986. A Pennsylvania law required doctors to tell a pregnant woman considering abortion about the possibility that harmful physical and psychological effects could be caused by the abortion procedure. The physician also had to give the woman information about agencies that could help her if she decided to give birth, and about the physical characteristics of her unborn child at two-week intervals.

The Court, in a narrow 5 to 4 ruling, overturned the Pennsylvania law on the grounds that it improperly restricted and discouraged women seeking to end their pregnancies. Justice Blackmun, who had written the Court's *Roe* opinion, again spoke for the majority. "The states are not free," said Blackmun, "under the guise of protecting maternal health or potential life, to intimidate women into continuing pregnancies."

In dissent, Justice Byron R. White strongly opposed the Court defining "fundamental" liberties "that are nowhere mentioned in the Constitution." White maintained that instead of imposing "its own controversial choices of value[s] on the people," the Court should return such hotly debated moral and political issues to the legislatures where elected representatives can express the public will.

In 1988, the Supreme Court dealt with a case involving anti-abortion picketers and the right to privacy. Pro-life picketers had gathered outside the home of obstetrician Dr. Benjamin Victoria in the town of Brookfield, Wisconsin. They shouted slogans such as: "Dr. Victoria, you're a killer." This prompted the town council to pass an ordinance making it unlawful for any person to engage in picketing outside the residence or dwelling of any individual in Brookfield.

Some of the picketers sued, claiming that the ordinance deprived them of their rights to freedom of speech. Attorneys for Brookfield argued that the measure was lawful because it did not prohibit all picketing but merely regulated it.

By a 6 to 3 vote, the Supreme Court sided with the town. Justice Sandra Day O'Connor, writing for the majority, explained that the Brookfield ordinance was valid because it protected the "right of residential privacy" by forbidding demonstrations targeted directly at the doctor and his family. "There simply is no right to force speech into the home of an unwilling listener," O'Connor concluded.

Eleven

RIGHTS of YOUTH

For many years juveniles accused of crimes were tried in the same courts and sentenced to the same prisons as adults. Children as young as seven sometimes were given long prison terms and occasionally even death sentences. One eight-year-old child was convicted and hanged for setting a barn on fire.

In the late 1800s, social reformers became concerned about the harsh treatment of juveniles who committed crimes. They believed that cases of young lawbreakers should be heard in special courts that did not operate under the same regulations as those found in adult courts. The first juvenile court was established in 1899 in Chicago, Illinois, and served as a model that was quickly followed by almost every state.

The idea behind the juvenile court was that it would act as a "protective parent" instead of a prosecutor. The goal would be rehabilitation rather than punishment of the young offender. In an adult criminal case, there is a formal public trial with specific rules, lawyers, and juries, and a set range of punishments for each type of crime. In a juvenile court, all proceedings would be informal and private; there would be no lawyers or juries; punishment would be assessed in terms of what would be just for each individual after careful consideration of the person's background and the circumstances pertaining to the criminal act. Juvenile lawbreakers might be placed on probation, taken from their families and put in foster homes, or sent to a reform school or state institution for delinquent youth.

Removing juvenile cases from the criminal court system benefited young people in many ways, but it also handicapped them in other ways. The traditional protections that adults have under the Bill of Rights and the Fourteenth Amendment did not apply to the juvenile court system. Young people were not guaranteed such rights as due process of law, assistance of counsel, a jury trial, cross-examination of witnesses, protection against self-incrimination, and the opportunity to appeal a court verdict to higher courts.

This absence of constitutional rights for juveniles came to the attention of the Supreme Court in 1967 in the landmark case of *In re Gault*. (The term *In re* means "in the matter of" or "concerning.") Gerald Gault, a fifteen-year-old boy in Arizona, was accused of making a lewd phone call to a Mrs. Cook, who lived in the neighborhood. Gault was arrested and turned over to the juvenile court without being given the opportunity to exercise any of the constitutional rights that an adult would have had in the same situation.

Gault's parents were not immediately told of the charges or given proper notice that their son would be hailed before a juvenile court judge. The boy was not told that he could remain silent or have a lawyer. The judge directly questioned Gault, who admitted that he had dialed Mrs. Cook's phone number, but insisted that a friend of his had made the vulgar remarks. Mrs. Cook did not testify at the hearing, so Gault had no chance to confront his accuser or have her cross-examined. At the conclusion of the informal hearing, the judge announced that Gault was a "juvenile delinquent" and sentenced him to serve six years at the State Industrial School. If Gault had been an adult, the maximum penalty for the alleged offense would have been a fine of fifty dollars or imprisonment for two months.

Gault's parents, who were appalled at the punishment and the court procedure, hired an attorney. Even though Arizona law prohibited appeals in juvenile cases, the attorney found a way to bring the case before the federal courts.

When the Court heard this case, the justices voted 8 to 1 in favor of Gault. Justice Abe Fortas, writing the majority opinion, declared that "neither the Fourteenth Amendment nor the Bill of Rights is for adults alone. . . . We are to treat the child as an individual human being and not revert in spite of good intentions to the more primitive days when he was treated as chattel [a personal possession]."

As a result of the *Gault* decision, minors acquired some but not all of the protections guaranteed by the Bill of Rights. Youth were given the following rights: (1) to receive the notice of charges sufficiently in advance of the scheduled court hearing to prepare an adequate defense; (2) to have a lawyer defend them at the hearing; (3) to be notified that they may remain silent and protect themselves against self-incrimination; and (4) to confront their accusers and have witnesses cross-examined.

Other constitutional rights of adult defendants were not extended by the *Gault* ruling to young people. In fact, in a 1971 decision *(McKeiver* v. *Pennsylvania)*, the Supreme Court declared that juveniles do not have the right to a jury trial. Justice Harry A. Blackmun explained that if all the procedures followed in adult criminal cases were injected into the juvenile court system, there would be little need for its separate existence. The jury trial, Blackmun reasoned, would bring with it the traditional delay, the formality and clamor of lawyers contesting each other, and the publicity that would make the trial a public affair instead of a private proceeding designed primarily to reform rather than punish juvenile offenders.

In 1975, the Court decided another issue pertaining to juveniles. Dwight Lopez was suspended from high school for ten days for allegedly taking part in a lunchroom disturbance that caused damage to some school property. Lopez had received no hearing before his suspension, and he claimed that this was a violation of the Fourteenth Amendment's due process clause.

The Supreme Court, by a vote of 5 to 4, agreed with Lopez and ordered that students facing suspension must be given some kind of hearing and an opportunity to present their side of the story. "Young people do not shed their rights at the schoolhouse door," said Justice Byron R. White for the majority, adding that "the Fourteenth Amendment as now applied to the States protects citizens against the State and all its creatures—Boards of Education not excepted."

Another case arising from a school situation was settled by the Supreme Court in 1978. For defying a teacher's order, James Ingraham, a junior high school student in Florida, received more than twenty licks with a paddle. The boy required medical attention and stayed out of school for eleven days.

Through his parents, Ingraham sued the school authorities, asking the court for damages. His lawyer claimed that paddling a student violated the Eighth Amendment protection against cruel and unusual punishment. He also insisted that the failure to give notice and hold a hearing before the punishment was inflicted were violations of the due process clause of the Fourteenth Amendment. The school officials, on the other hand, argued that corporal punishment was permitted by nearly all of the states, including Florida. They said it often provided an effective way to discipline students and maintain a learning environment in the schools.

The Supreme Court, by another close vote in *Ingraham* v. *Wright* (5 to 4), upheld the right of school authorities to paddle students. Justice Lewis F. Powell, Jr., speaking for the majority, said that ". . . the State itself may impose such corporal punishment as is necessary for the proper education of the child and for the maintenance of group discipline." Powell asserted that the "school child has little need for the protection of the Eighth Amendment [because] . . . the openness of the public school and its supervision by the community afford significant safeguards against the kinds of abuses from which the Eighth Amendment protects the prisoner."

In dissent, Justice Byron R. White took issue with the opinion of the majority that corporal punishment is never limited by the Eighth Amendment. "Where corporal punishment becomes so severe as to be unacceptable in a civilized society," White wrote, "I can see no reason that it should become any more acceptable just because it is inflicted on children in the public schools."

In 1985, the Court heard a case involving the warrantless search of a high school girl's purse; the search produced marijuana. The girl claimed that this search and seizure by school personnel were illegal intrusions on her Fourth Amendment rights. The justices had to decide in this case whether the right of the school administrators to enforce school rules and maintain discipline outweighed the student's right to privacy.

The Supreme Court, by a 6 to 3 vote, sided with the school authorities. Justice White, who in *Ingraham* had opposed corporal punishment in schools, this time supported the position of the school officials. Speaking for the majority, he observed that drug use had become a major social problem, and, as a result of society's need to combat this problem, "it is evident that the school setting requires some easing of the restrictions to which searches by public authorities are ordinarily subject."

Another landmark case that tested the power of school authorities was decided by the Supreme Court in 1988. The case, *Hazelwood School District* v. *Kuhlmeier*, pertained to a student newspaper called *Spectrum*, that was produced by journalism students at Hazelwood East High School near St. Louis, Missouri. In May 1983, Principal

Robert Reynolds ordered two articles deleted from the paper. One told about the experiences of three Hazelwood students who were pregnant; the names of the students did not appear in the story. The other article discussed the impact of parental divorce on teenagers. In removing the articles from the newspaper, Reynolds said he believed the students discussed in the stories were identifiable and the material was "inappropriate and unsuitable" reading for teenagers.

Three students who wrote for *Spectrum* brought suit, alleging a violation of their First Amendment rights to freedom of speech and freedom of the press. A federal trial judge ruled against the students, but the 8th Circuit Court of Appeals reversed the decision, affirming that *Spectrum* was a "public forum" because it was intended to be and operated as a vehicle for student opinion.

By a 5 to 3 vote, the Supreme Court ruled that the principal had not violated student rights by deleting the articles. The students had no legal authority to publish the

Above: *Journalism students of the Hazelwood East High School newspaper,* Spectrum, *in 1988— immediately after the Supreme Court's ruling against the publication of controversial articles appearing five years earlier in the paper.* Below: *One of the three journalism students who sued school officials. Five years after the articles appeared, she is shown as a university student reacting to the Court's ruling.*

controversial articles, the Court said, because the paper was owned and controlled by the school. Writing for the majority, Justice Byron R. White declared, "We hold that educators do not offend the First Amendment by exercising control over the style and content of student speech in school-sponsored expressive activities so long as their actions are reasonably related to legitimate pedagogical concerns."

Justice William J. Brennan, Jr., in a dissent joined by Justices Thurgood Marshall and Harry A. Blackmun, vigorously rejected the notion that school-sponsored speech was less worthy of protection than any other. He argued that the new ruling might permit school officials to censor anything that personally offended them. "The young men and women of Hazelton East expected a civics lesson," he wrote, "but not the one the court teaches them today."

The Bill of Rights still has the same words that James Madison and his colleagues penned in 1789. But as times have changed during the past two hundred years, so have the views of the Supreme Court, which is the ultimate guardian of these rights. The Bill of Rights is living law—vital, dynamic, and flexible enough to meet the new challenges of our modern world. It guards our most cherished freedoms today and will continue to do so for ages to come.

Source notes

Chapter 1

1. Page Smith, *The Shaping of America* (New York: McGraw-Hill, 1980), p. 94.
2. *Washington Post*, May 7, 1987, p. 18.
3. Bernard Schwartz, *The Great Rights of Mankind: A History of the American Bill of Rights* (New York: Oxford University Press), p. 104.
4. *Ibid.*, p. 120.
5. Milton Lomask, *The Spirit of 1787: The Making of Our Constitution* (New York: Farrar Straus Giroux, 1980), p. 189.
6. Schwartz, *op. cit.* p. vii.

Chapter 2

1. James Madison, ''Memorial and Remonstrances against Religious Assessments,'' as quoted in the *Los Angeles Times*, December 22, 1984, Part II, p. 8.

Chapter 3

1. Paul C. Bartholomew and Joseph F. Menez, *Summaries of Leading Cases on the Constitution* (Totowa, N.J.: Rowman & Allanheld, 1983), p. 279.

Chapter 4

1. *The Supreme Court and Individual Rights* (Washington: Congressional Quarterly Inc., 1980), p. 79.

2. "Religion, Morality and American Education," *Bill of Rights in Action* (Los Angeles: Constitutional Rights Foundation, February/March, 1983), p. 22.

Chapter 7

1. "The Citizen in de Tocqueville's America," *Bill of Rights in Action* (Los Angeles: Constitutional Rights Foundation, Fall, 1985), p. 2.

Chapter 10

1. "Privacy and Your Rights," *Bill of Rights in Action* (Los Angeles: Constitutional Rights Foundation, September, 1979), p. 18.

For further reading

More information about the Supreme Court cases discussed in this book can be found in *Summaries of Leading Cases on the Constitution* by Paul C. Bartholomew and Joseph F. Menez, *Bill of Rights Reader: Leading Constitutional Cases* by Milton R. Konvitz, *The Supreme Court and Individual Rights* by Congressional Quarterly Inc., and *These Liberties: Case Studies in Civil Rights* by Rocco J. Tresolini. Many of the other books mentioned below also contain information on specific Supreme Court cases.

Bartholomew, Paul C. and Joseph F. Menez. *Summaries of Leading Cases on the Constitution*. Totowa, N.J.: Rowman & Allanheld, 1983.

Brant, Irving. *The Bill of Rights; Its Origin and Meaning*. Indianapolis: Bobbs-Merrill, 1965.

Burns, James MacGregor. *The Vineyard of Liberty*. New York: Knopf, 1982.

Cox, Archibald. *The Court and the Constitution*. Boston: Houghton Mifflin, 1987.

David, Andrew. *Famous Supreme Court Cases*. Minneapolis: Lerner, 1980.

Forte, David F. *The Supreme Court*. New York: Watts, 1979.

Friendly, Fred W. and Martha J.H. Elliott. *The Constitution: That Delicate Balance*. New York: Random House, 1984.

Goode, Stephen. *The Controversial Court: Supreme Court Influences on American Life*. New York: Messner, 1982.

————. *The Right to Privacy.* New York: Watts, 1983.

Hentoff, Nat. *The First Freedom: The Tumultuous History of Free Speech in America.* New York: Dell, 1981.

Kohn, Bernice. *The Spirit and the Letter: The Struggle for Rights in America.* New York: Viking, 1974.

Konvitz, Milton R. *Bill of Rights Reader: Leading Constitutional Cases.* Ithaca, N.Y.: Cornell University Press, 1973.

Lindop, Edmund. *Birth of the Constitution.* Hillside, N.J.: Enslow, 1987.

————. *By a Single Vote! One-Vote Decisions That Changed American History.* Harrisburg, Pa.: Stackpole, 1987.

Miller, Helen Hill. *The Case for Liberty.* Chapel Hill, N.C.: University of North Carolina Press, 1965.

Morris, Richard B. *Witnesses at the Creation.* New York: Holt, Rinehart and Winston, 1985.

Schwartz, Bernard. *The Great Rights of Mankind: A History of the American Bill of Rights.* New York: Oxford University Press, 1977.

Schwartz, Herman, ed. *The Burger Years: Rights and Wrongs in the Supreme Court, 1969–1986.* New York: Penguin Books, 1988.

Sgroi, Peter. *Blue Jeans and Black Robes: Teenagers and the Supreme Court.* New York: Messner, 1979.

Starr, Isidore. *Justice: Due Process of Law.* St. Paul: West, 1981.

————. *The Idea of Liberty: First Amendment Freedoms.* St. Paul: West, 1980.

The Supreme Court and Individual Rights. Washington: Congressional Quarterly Inc., 1980.

Tresolini, Rocco J. *These Liberties: Case Studies in Civil Rights.* Philadelphia: Lippincott, 1968.

Warren, Earl. *A Republic, If You Can Keep It.* New York: Quadrangle Books, 1972.

Index